—— THE ——
ONE-NUMBER
—— BUDGET ——

THE
ONE-NUMBER
BUDGET

Why Traditional
Budgets Fail and What
to Do About It

JOHN W. CRANE

TENJAN

The One-Number Budget
Why Traditional Budgets Fail and What to Do About It

ISBN 978-1-5445-3365-0 Hardcover
     978-1-5445-3366-7 Paperback
     978-1-5445-3367-4 Ebook

To my wife, Linda,

and my daughter, Emma,

who are the greatest blessings

that any man could

ever hope for.

I love you.

CONTENTS

INTRODUCTION

Have you ever seen *Moneyball*?

That's the movie where Brad Pitt plays Billy Beane, the longtime general manager of the Oakland A's. It's based on the book of the same title written by Michael Lewis. This movie is one of my all-time favorites, and I've seen it 15 or 20 times.

Okay, maybe that's a little embarrassing, and I should watch a little less Netflix. But I can't help it. I love this movie.

There's a really special scene where Peter Brand, played by Jonah Hill, is talking to Billy Beane on his first day of work with the A's. Peter is an economist who has been hired by the team to take a massive amount of statistical data gathered about every single player in Major League Baseball, analyze it, and evaluate who should be brought onto the team without busting the team's small-market salary budget. We're talking about all of the statistics you'd find on the back of baseball cards, plus thousands of other numbers and metrics.

There's a pivotal moment where Peter says, "It's about getting things down to one number. Using the stats the way we read them, we'll find value in players that no one else can see. People are overlooked for a variety of biased reasons and perceived flaws: age, appearance, personality."

It's about getting things down to one number.

If we can just get things down to one number, it's easier to make decisions. Reducing complexity helped the A's hire great players and get to the playoffs on a shoestring budget, and their system changed baseball forever.

One night as I was rewatching *Moneyball* to unwind, I sat straight up at this scene and hit the pause button.

What if I could remove the frustration and tedium from the traditional budgeting process and get the whole thing down to just one number? If people only had one thing to think about instead of trying to track 30 or more line items, they could finally get somewhere with their finances.

As a financial advisor, I had spent 15 years struggling to help clients manage their cash flow. I tried coaching them through traditional budgets to track income and expenses. I gave them homework that required them to weed through their credit card bills and categorize expenses each month. I spent time scaring them into thinking their money was scarce in an attempt to get them to save more.

This all came to a head with a couple—I'll call them Mike and Lauren —who I had worked with for years. Their income kept going up, but their savings rate kept going down. They just couldn't bring themselves to increase their savings and investments when they got raises and promotions, and they were actually saving a smaller percentage of their income each year.

This was upsetting to me, because I desperately wanted to help them be ready for retirement. They were great people, but no matter what I tried, I couldn't get them to increase their savings. I could see the writing on the wall, and it wasn't pretty: they would have to work until they died if they kept going this way.

One day, I took Mike out to lunch. I had tried everything, and this was my last-ditch effort to get him to see the light. I sat him down and was completely transparent. "Look," I said, "I feel like I'm failing you because I can't deliver this message about your savings in a way that you can hear and act on. I don't know what to do. How can I get you to understand and move forward in a way that won't leave you broke?"

It was a tense conversation.

THE PROBLEM

Mike and Lauren's problem is everybody's problem: traditional budgeting is too time-consuming, and it doesn't work for most people. There are just too many variables to track, from putting gas in the car to groceries in your cart. And you can't just do a budget once and call it a day, either. You have to constantly update and adjust as your numbers change.

It's exhausting. No one wants to work all day, help the kids with homework, and then, instead of actually having a moment to relax with their spouse, spend the evening sorting through expenses and deciding what changes to make to get the monthly budget to come out even.

It's also disheartening. I work with a lot of couples, and it's so easy to have a budget discussion turn into a prosecution/defense of individual purchases. That's a recipe for conflict and unhappiness. It also doesn't help that people are constantly bombarded by all sorts of financial talking heads scolding them for buying a latte or taking a vacation, shouting out all sorts of confusing, contradictory advice.

And perhaps the biggest problem of all is that traditional budgets provide only a snapshot of your finances, rather than the long view of cash flow over your lifetime. This is the single hardest concept for me to teach clients, and it was what Mike and Lauren couldn't wrap their heads around. You probably struggle with this, too—and you may not even realize it.

THE SOLUTION

Because complexity is killing people's ability to manage their money effectively over their lifetime, I knew I had to get things down to one number. *The One-Number Budget* helps reduce complexity and gives you one number to manage to each month. It also prioritizes a lifetime perspective of cash flow to make sure your future self doesn't suffer for a lack of vision today. Best of all, it's easy to implement so you can get started on the path to building wealth *today*.

In this book, you will learn to cut through the noise of traditional financial advice to get to your One Number. Specifically, you will understand:

» How to give your future self a seat at the table when making financial decisions

» Why complicated monthly budgets fail

» Your Human Life Value and how this number can help guide your planning

» How to manage your cash flow over a lifetime, not just month-to-month

» How to put wealth building first

» How to find your One Number

» How to manage your spending to live within your One Number

» How to avoid common spending pitfalls

» How to balance family members' needs within your One Number

» How to recognize and address psychological barriers to saving

» How your vision of the future brings your One Number to life

WHY I WROTE THIS BOOK

I spent the first 10 years of my adult life chasing paychecks and promotions. By the time I was 29 years old, I had my master of business administration, a nice house and car, and was just named a senior national account manager at a major telecom company. The company sent me to Tuscaloosa, Alabama, to shadow Tom, the man I would be replacing when he retired the following month.

We met early one morning at the Waffle House near my hotel to go over the day's accounts and action plan. We each slid into our booth seats at the same moment, and it was weirdly like looking into a mirror. All of a sudden, I had this tunnel vision moment where everything went fuzzy around the edges. I could see Tom's lips moving, but I couldn't hear a word he was saying.

In that moment, I knew in a flash that, even though there was only two and a half feet of table separating us, the distance between us couldn't have been greater. Tom was 65 and I was only 29, which meant I still had 36 years to go to get to the retirement side of the table. Tom was happy, but I definitely was not. I already knew that I didn't like this job, and that there was no way I was going to make it to his side of the table.

I quit and became a financial advisor instead.

Why was I so miserable in the big corporate job? I never felt like what I did there mattered. I wanted to be able to help people directly, not just sell data contracts to hospitals. I wanted to see the impact of my work and help make people's lives better.

I could have written a book about investing in the markets or insurance strategies, but I picked budgeting instead. That's because I have seen firsthand how the One-Number Budget has changed people's lives and empowered them to manage their money for their whole lifetime. I wrote this book to bring the One-Number Budget out into the world so that it can help thousands of people.

I wrote it to help *you*.

This book isn't a traditional personal financial lecture that tells you to give up your Starbucks' habit or tries to shame you into saving money by criticizing your credit and spending habits. I'm not your parent, and I have no interest in telling you how to live your life or spend your money. That's up to you.

So what *does* this book do? It treats you like you're one of my clients and gives you a real roadmap to plan for the future—not just for the next month or year, but for the next 30 to 60 years. It provides an easy-to-use tool to help you stay on track day-to-day, week-to-week, and month-to-month. It simplifies the budgeting process to put savings first and explain lifetime cash flow in a way that will help change how you think about your income forever. And it teaches you not just to calculate your One Number, but also to help protect it by working to avoid the most common pitfalls and potholes that people encounter on the road to retirement.

No matter where you are right now, you can take steps to manage your cash flow and start building wealth. It all starts with making sure your future self has a seat at the table when you sit down to create your financial plan.

Chapter 1

THE THIEF

When I was young I spent my days
driving fast and dining well.
The life I lived felt so complete—
an endless pleasure carousel.

I earned my pay so easily
the money flowed into my hand.
And my best friend made life a joy
by building me a wonderland.

"You've worked too hard to not enjoy
all the best your wealth can buy:
Fine wine, resorts, and sports cars, too!"
He raised my standards to the sky.

Those days were gold! But now they're gone.
I sit here tired, broke, alone.
Too old to work, my best days past.
I can't go back—the time has flown.

What of the friend who cheered me on,
advising this too-willing hearer
to spend until it was too late?
I see him only in the mirror.

—JOHN W. CRANE

ARE YOU A THIEF?

If I asked you if you would ever steal money from an old person, leaving them destitute in their golden years, you would be horrified at the thought. Of course you would never do that! It's cruel and immoral.

While stealing from someone else is obviously wrong, many people are all too willing to commit this crime against themselves. The easiest person to steal from is your future self, and if you don't plan ahead, you will rationalize your way into a retirement that doesn't live up to your expectations—if you're even able to retire at all.

I was inspired to start this chapter with a poem because I have met with many couples over the years who come to me in pain. In this hypothetical example, a couple in their mid-fifties comes into my office because they have decided that it's finally time to get serious about their financial planning. They're calm and polite, but as they sit down across from me, I can see fear in their eyes.

That's because they have already realized they're broke.

They probably haven't ever said it out loud to anyone—not even each other—but they've realized that they have a net worth of about $250,000 between their home equity and their 401(k) balances. At best, they have only 10 or 15 more years of work in them. They know they're in trouble, and they don't know what to do.

Still, they've come to me because I'm a professional, and they're hoping that I have a magic wand to fix this and get them on a pace to retire comfortably. I'm not a magician, but I do have a calculator, and I want to help.

So we crunch the numbers to find that they make about $200,000 per year combined, and they're spending almost all of it, either outright or to pay down credit card debt from past spending. They might be putting 5 to 6 percent into their 401(k) to capture their company's matching funds, but they have no real savings outside of that. They've been doing this for years.

Here's where I have to look them in the eye and tell them that, to maybe be able to make it to a decent retirement in a couple decades, they'll need to slash their expenses and start saving 50 to 60 percent of their income right now.

They glance at each other, then back to me. I can see in their faces that they can't process this information. "We could never do that," they say.

I want to help, so I work to get them to see the reality built into their numbers. With the $250,000 they currently have saved, the best they can hope to draw in retirement is about $10,000 per year. Add that to a potential $40,000 per year in Social Security income between the two of them, and they've got $50,000 to live on in retirement—a *75 percent reduction* in income from their current $200,000.

"Oh, that's fine," they say. "No worries! We can get by on $50,000, no problem." And they get up, shake my hand, and leave my office, never to return.

Of course, this doesn't make any sense. What they can't see—and really don't want to see—is that refusing to do the hard work now doesn't get them out of it. Instead, it just pushes the moment of reckoning into the future. But they *will* have to live with substantially reduced income at some point.

This is so sad, and it's one of the hardest parts of my job.

Why do they do this? Because it's just too painful to face the truth. Instead, they choose denial. They put a mental wall between their present selves, who can't live on less than $200,000 per year, and their future selves, who they assume will be fine on $50,000. They steal from their future selves to avoid making painful changes to their lives today.

This is a heartbreaking situation, and I see it all too often. Don't let your future self become a victim of theft.

INCREMENTAL THEFT

I want to be very clear that couples like the one described above aren't stupid, selfish, or greedy. They don't even live particularly extravagant lifestyles. These people don't all own boats or have a three-car garage filled with Mercedes sedans. Over the course of many years, they steal from themselves *incrementally*.

This happens in many ways. Maybe it's with impulse purchases from the checkout line at Target. Maybe it's the lure of a new car when the old one still has plenty of good years left in it. It's common to get into a habit of rationalizing increased spending as your current self turns things that are really just wants into needs that must be met today.

This happens a lot at the car dealership, for example. If your current payment is $350 per month, it's pretty easy to rationalize trading in your old car for a much better one. The new monthly payment is $500, and that's only $150 extra. That's not much at all!

And so it goes, with hundreds of little decisions that add up to grand larceny against your future self. Looking at things month by month feels fine, and you get a rush of pleasure from the shiny new object. But when you look at that monthly expense over the course of 20 or 30 years, it's a disaster. The monthly budget snapshot is comforting, but it's not the whole picture.

This is how the old man in the poem ended up broke in the end, too. He was happy to spend his money enjoying life in his youth, but without a plan for the future, he now faces a life in which all of his pleasures are in the past. The sad irony is that he stole from himself—and he'll have to live with the consequences of that theft for the rest of his life.

The whole concept of the future self is a pretty new one, which helps to explain why it's so hard to act upon. I've never been really big on studying history, but I am surrounded by it. I live in Alexandria, Virginia, a city with a tremendous amount of history that tracks right along with the founding of our country. This is where George Washington was from. As you enter Alexandria, there's a sign that lets you know it was founded in 1749.

Passing that sign one day got me thinking about what life was like back then. What was it like to live here during the Revolution and then during the Civil War? In 1860, the average life expectancy was about 40.[1] Back then, there was no future self to worry about—you were almost certainly never going to have to worry about outliving your money. You were in survival mode to earn what you needed to live. You did your best to accumulate what you could for your comfort and maybe to pass something on to your heirs.

It wasn't until life expectancy started to take off in the twentieth century that we had a thing called retirement. The whole idea is a pretty new concept that's probably less than 100 years old. From a psychological standpoint, that means we haven't really evolved to catch up with the idea of saving for a period of our lives in which we no longer work. We're built to avoid pain and get what we can now, just as our hunter-gatherer ancestors gorged when food was available—they never knew when their next meal would be delayed by conditions outside of their control.

Unfortunately, that instinct doesn't serve your future self very well these days. To make sure you don't fall victim to your own thievery, you need to give your future self a seat at the table for all of your financial decision-making.

---

[1] O'Neill, Aaron. "Life expectancy in the United States, 1860-2020." Statista. 3 February 2021. https://www.statista.com/statistics/1040079/life-expectancy-united-states-all-time/.

THE LESSON

Don't rationalize away serious financial concerns or leave them to figure out later. The time to build and protect your wealth is *now*.

You don't have to end up like the old man in the poem. It's within your power to make changes today to stop stealing from your future self and get on track for the retirement you deserve.

And if you happen to identify with the couple I described earlier, you can still benefit from the One-Number Budget. It's never too late to make changes that will help your future self live a happier, more comfortable life. This journey is for everyone, and we'll tackle the problems that lead to theft one by one throughout the book.

One of the biggest ways we steal from our future selves is by failing to plan—even if we think we're on track with a monthly budget.

Chapter 2

WHY TRADITIONAL BUDGETING METHODS DON'T ALWAYS WORK

If you've picked up this book, it's probably because you already know deep down that traditional budgets don't really work. If they haven't worked in the past for you, you're not alone. And it's not even your fault. The problem lies with the budgeting process itself.

To better understand the problem, imagine yourself behind the wheel of your car. You're driving along, lost in thought, when all of a sudden the dashboard lights up, bells are going off, and you see that your gas light is on. The needle is on E. You're running on empty.

On this particular trip, you're nowhere near home. The road stretches out as far as you can see, and you have to hope that you'll get to a gas station before you run out of fuel. I know just how this feels, because

I've been there. That creeping feeling of panic starts to move up from your gut into your throat. There's nothing worse than white-knuckling the steering wheel, hoping you can get to the next gas station.

Hopefully you'll have just enough gas to get you there, but what do you do in the meantime? Everything you can to conserve gas. You turn off the radio and the air conditioner, and you start paying really close attention to how you're driving in hopes of maximizing fuel efficiency. If there's a downhill, you put the car in neutral to coast for as long as you can. Every driver's ed trick you've ever learned is on the table here, because it's an emergency.

And then, in the distance, you see a sign for a gas station. You pull over, turn off the engine, and let out a big sigh of relief. You made it, and you're safe. Whew!

So what happens next? You fill up the tank, pull out of the gas station, and blast the air conditioning. Maybe you even roll the windows down at the same time, just because you can. You crank up the radio, put your foot on the gas, and speed down the highway to make up for lost time. You're feeling great—and you're burning fuel a whole lot faster than you were when you thought you were going to run out just a few moments earlier.

Here's the point: when you feel like you have lots of resources, like that tank of gas is full and there are plenty of places to refuel ahead, you operate your car differently. You're not as concerned about efficiency, because everything is good. It's only when you're feeling the pinch that you start to worry about conserving fuel and stretching your resources out to last as long as possible. The unexpected emergency is what drives action, but by then it may be too late—and who wants to leave things up to luck?

TRADITIONAL BUDGETS ARE
ONLY A SNAPSHOT

Traditional budgets fail because they only provide a shortsighted, month-by-month look at your finances. They ignore the long-term view of lifetime cash flow, and they often push savings to the bottom of the monthly to-do list.

It's a lot like that tank of gas, in that a standard budget only gives you a sense of whether your tank is full or empty. Do you have enough to get to the next gas station, or don't you? But that doesn't answer the bigger question of whether you'll have enough fuel to get you through your whole road trip. You feel fine when the tank is full, so you enjoy yourself—right up until the needle hits empty.

Budgets are a lot like that. When you're in your prime earning years, it's easy to feel flush with cash. Your bank account, like that gas tank, is full! Why not make yourself comfortable and reward yourself for all your hard work by spending some of that money? After all, you're working hard, and the paychecks show up every two weeks to replenish your account. It's as if you've been guaranteed a gas station every 20 miles on your road trip.

Of course, not all roads have that many gas stations, and not all periods of your life come with a paycheck. Right now you've been trained to rely on that biweekly paycheck and think only about getting through the two weeks between them. But someday the checks will stop coming. At that point, you'll either have savings to rely on, or you'll have to white-knuckle your way through while frantically cutting back on everything that made the ride enjoyable in the first place.

When it comes to money, context is everything. If I gave you a million dollars today, would that make you rich?

If you knew you only had another 30 days to live, then yes. You'd be truly wealthy, because you'd be unlikely to spend it all before you died. You could do whatever you wanted to with that money and never have to worry about it running out.

But if your crystal ball said you were going to live for another 30 *years*? Well, now maybe you're not so rich after all. That amount may or may not be enough to get you through three more decades, and you'd have a whole list of decisions to make about your lifestyle to decide whether or not it's enough.

Context is everything.

We've all been taught to think about a budget in terms of months. Figure out how much money you'll earn in a month, make sure you keep your expenses low enough to get to the next month, and you're all good. But here's the thing. The short-term snapshot that a monthly budget provides doesn't show you the big picture of your lifetime, so it's not the best tool to help you make good decisions about your money.

Yet everywhere you turn, you're being marketed to in a way that prioritizes a monthly snapshot over your long-term financial health. This happens in advertising and sales all the time, and it's easy to see why: a monthly payment is a much smaller number than the full cost of a house, car, or other major purchase. A $450 payment every month for five years will always be an easier sell than a lump sum of $25,000.

When costs are presented in terms of a monthly payment, you're much more likely to say, "Sure, I can do that. It's just a little bit more each month." You're only human, and it's much easier to deal with small numbers and a shorter time frame than it is to think about how your cash flow today needs to last for decades. Remember, the whole idea of providing for rather than stealing from your future self is a new one, and it's not natural for most people to think so far ahead.

But here's the truth about your income. One day you will stop working, whether you choose to or not. On that day, the income will permanently stop, and you will have to rely on the wealth you've built to carry you through the rest of your life. Traditional monthly budgets often lull people into a false sense of security by making them feel that things are balanced right now, but they don't help project into the future to see just how much is being stolen from our future selves when we decide to spend that $450 extra each month instead of saving and investing it.

TRADITIONAL BUDGETS MAKE YOU FEEL LIKE A FAILURE

That false sense of security feels good for a while, but it only lasts as long as your monthly budget is in balance. Anyone who has tried to keep up with a household budget for more than a few months knows that the balancing act doesn't last for long.

Most people start the budgeting process with excellent intentions. They want to get organized and take charge of their finances, so they hit the internet and print out a general household budget. There are hundreds of them out there, and they ask you to list out everything you could ever imagine spending money on: the mortgage, utilities, cable TV, food, car payments, childcare.

The list goes on. And on and on and on, breaking categories down into subcategories until your head is spinning as you try to figure out exactly how much you spend on lattes each month. You do your best and assign numbers to all 20 or 30 categories of expenditures, and it looks great. You did your homework by figuring out the average of what you spent on each item for the last six months, and your new household budget is a work of art. You may even sit there admiring it when you think no one is watching.

Then all of a sudden, from somewhere behind you, you hear a sound. Is it raining? There's a drip, drip, drip coming from somewhere, but it turns out it's inside the house. Your ceiling is leaking, and you realize that there's a leak in the upstairs bathroom. Water is flowing from the second floor onto the first, and you glance back at the budget you felt so good about only a moment ago. The line for household repairs has $50 budgeted, because things don't usually break.

Three days and countless full buckets of water later, the plumber hands you a bill for $750 for the repair. That beautiful budget is blown not just for the month, but for the next year and a half. Now you need to start all over, adjusting every line item to accommodate the new reality. And you'll have to do it again and again.

The problem with snapshots is that they only mark one moment in time, and there's always an outlier expense that throws the whole thing for a loop. This isn't your fault. It's just how life works. Get hit with enough curveballs in your budget, though, and it's pretty easy to end up feeling like a failure—and even easier to want to give up on the whole thing.

But I'm here to tell you that you are not a failure. Traditional budgets are failing *you*.

TRADITIONAL BUDGETS ARE
TOO TIME-CONSUMING

Americans are busier than ever. I know in my household, my wife and I both have challenging jobs, and we're busy juggling our own schedules along with our child's school day and activities. There's barely enough time to enjoy dinner together, much less a leisurely evening just hanging out. Most of my clients are in the same boat. Maybe you are, too.

So when we finally get an hour or two alone at the end of the day, the last thing we want to do is log into our bank accounts to go over the budget. Who wants to flip through the latest credit card statement and categorize expenses to make sure you didn't go over in some categories or end up with money to spare in others?

As we saw with the unexpected plumbing bill, maintaining a household budget requires constant attention. It takes real work to keep up with the changes and to make sure you're on track—or can adjust to roll with the punches. There are apps and tools out there that can help streamline the process, but at the end of the day, it's up to you to sit down every week and review your income and expenses to make sure you're actually following the roadmap you created when you first filled in all those numbers.

The thing about a traditional monthly budget is that it's a process, not a product. You can't just look at it once a year and think you've done the job. For a traditional budget to work, you have to review and update it and remain vigilant *all the time*. And that takes so much effort that it's just not practical for most people to do it well.

Technology has made it easier than ever to spend, thanks to apps like Venmo and others that make it so easy to buy things. When your credit card is already in your Amazon account, all you have to do is push a button. The more ways you have to spend, the harder it is to keep track of where your money is going, which just adds to the time spent balancing those spending categories.

And when you're already tired, which is easier: checking your budget to see if you have enough money to eat out with friends at the end of the month, or putting the meal on your credit card and figuring it out later?

I can't remember the last time I heard one of my friends say, "Sorry, John, but I just checked our budget and we're a little behind. We'll have to do it next month instead." Checking the budget is a chore that takes so much of your energy that it feels more like a punishment than a helpful tool. No wonder people give up on them!

What about My Budgeting App?

Technology has made a lot of great things possible, and budgeting apps can take a lot of the tedium out of developing and maintaining a traditional budget. If you're already saving 20 percent of your income every month and your budgeting app feels like a helpful tool rather than a burden, keep doing what you're doing!

However, many people find that budgeting apps aren't a silver bullet for solving their financial problems. Like paper budgets, they require time to set up, and they'll only be useful if you keep checking in with them regularly to make sure you're staying on track. And even the best apps allow your savings to fall to the bottom of the list of priorities if you aren't vigilant.

Budgeting apps provide a great tactical solution for people who have no idea where their money is going. If you've never stopped to think about your spending, having your cash flow automatically tagged and sorted into spending categories can be eye-opening and a great start to getting a better handle on your finances. Once you have a good picture of your spending, you'll still need to work through all the psychology baked into your spending and saving.

TRADITIONAL BUDGETS TREAT
YOU LIKE A CHILD

When I first started out as a financial advisor, I used to help clients create a traditional budget all the time. I thought it was part of the job. We've all been conditioned to think that grown-ups have these perfect budgets all planned out, and I wanted to fulfill that responsibility with my clients.

But then I realized that some people would start to avoid coming to see me when it was time to pull out the budget for review. They were worried that I would judge them for their spending and tell them that they were wrong to want certain things. It's not surprising that they felt that way, since most of the talking heads on TV make a lot of money by scolding people about how they spend their money.

I started to make a big announcement at the beginning of every budgeting conversation to try to alleviate their fears. "When it comes to budgeting, my job is to give you the 10,000-foot view," I'd say. "I'm never going to point to any line item and tell you you're spending too much on restaurants. I'm not here to tell you that you are bad or wrong."

In the end, that speech didn't make much of a difference, because it's the traditional budget itself that is parental. It's a document that wags its finger at you and tells you what to do. Nobody likes being treated like a child. We all want to have the freedom to make our own choices—and the freedom to change our minds. Unfortunately, many people feel judged by the process of budgeting, so they end up rebelling. Of course, rebelling against your own budget only ends up hurting your future self.

Parental budgets also just aren't any fun. We all know what we *should* do, but it's difficult to embrace delayed gratification all the time. By accounting for every penny, traditional budgets are often so tightly drawn that they leave no room for spontaneity or enjoyment. Denying yourself fun treats or deserved vacations works against human nature, so it's bound to fail. Just like a too-strict parent who doesn't understand why their teenagers are suddenly pushing back, a too-stringent traditional budget can backfire and lead you to pickpocket your future self to afford a little bit of fun today.

TRADITIONAL BUDGETS PUT SAVINGS LAST

Most of the problems with traditional budgets have to do with human nature and the ways in which budgeting bumps up against our natural inclinations. But there's one major flaw that's all about the budget itself: your savings end up at the bottom of the list of priorities.

When you think about all the items on your household budget, your mind first goes to your biggest bills. These are nonnegotiables like the mortgage, utilities, food, and clothing. Bills to creditors come first, because there are real, immediate consequences for not meeting these obligations. Most traditional budget templates start with the biggest bills and basic needs at the top and prioritize spending in order from needs to wants.

Putting money into savings, on the other hand, feels much more negotiable than regular bills. Because saving money is paying our future self rather than a flesh-and-blood person who can shut off the electricity, it's very easy to push that line item farther and farther down the priority list. We start to negotiate with ourselves, promising that if we skimp on savings to pay for new shoes this month, we'll make it up later, maybe after we get a promotion. Do this often enough, and in 30 or 40 years you end up like the sad old man in our poem.

In fact, most people who use a traditional budget base their savings goals on the amount that they have leftover at the end of the month. Saving literally comes last, after everything else they need and want to spend their money on. This leads to far lower savings rates than what you need to have a comfortable retirement when life eventually forces you to stop working.

This is a huge weakness of the traditional budget, because your savings need to come *first*. It's a lot like looking after your health: if you don't make it a priority, you'll eventually rob your future self of a good life. I learned this the hard way years ago. When I was in my twenties, I had a personal rule that as long as I was under 200 pounds, I was okay. Specific diet and exercise didn't matter much if I just held steady.

When I hit my thirties, my doctor told me that my cholesterol was over 300 and I was at risk for a massive heart attack. Suddenly, my future self was staring back at me in the mirror, and I realized I needed to make sure that I got enough exercise. I finally figured out that if I waited until the end of a long workday, I would never, ever get to the gym. But if I get up early, put on my running shoes, and take care of it first thing in the morning, I get it done—and it actually feels good.

I solved my problem by moving exercise from the last thing on my daily list to the first. That's what the One-Number Budget does for wealth building. While traditional budgets push savings to the bottom of the list, the One-Number Budget puts your savings first.

THE LESSON

It's okay to call the traditional budget broken. If you've tried and failed to stick to a complicated household budget, you're not alone. Most people struggle with this because traditional budgets are too complicated and time-consuming to keep up with. They provide only a snapshot of your finances and make it difficult to visualize how decisions you make today will affect your future self. Worst of all, they tend to make saving an afterthought instead of the central goal of your financial life.

Given all these problems, why should you keep banging your head against the wall? You have my full permission to look at something else and try something new. If traditional budgets don't work for you, you need to find something that does so you can get on track for the future you deserve.

Remember that awful feeling of running on empty and having to hope for the good luck to get to the next gas station before getting stranded? In your car, you have the tools you need to track your fuel levels—but you also have to plan ahead for the trip. Otherwise, all you can do is hope that there will be another exit with a gas station. Maybe there will be, but maybe, one day, you'll end up stranded on the side of the road.

It's one thing to get stuck walking a few miles but another thing entirely to get stuck without enough money for the last decades of your life. Traditional budgets are like your gas gauge: they show you a snapshot of your resources, but they don't do anything to plan how to get from point A to point B.

So forget about the microscopic focus on the traditional monthly budget. Tear it up! Instead, let's zoom out to see the big picture of your whole life so we can figure out how much your financial gas tank actually holds.

Chapter 3

HUMAN LIFE VALUE

W hen I first started my new career as a financial advisor, my mentor worked with me for a full year before I was ready to take on clients of my own. When he finally felt I was ready, he let me work with several young couples. As a hypothetical example of this type of client, let's look at Nate and Laura.

Nate and Laura were a young couple just starting out. They were married and had good jobs, and they wanted to make sure they took care of their money so their future family would have everything they needed. I liked Nate and Laura a lot, and I very much wanted to do a good job for them.

Our first meeting was in the springtime, and I took them through the initial planning process. During this first meeting, I make sure that clients understand their insurance needs so they have the right protection in case something happens. No one likes to talk about life insurance because it forces you to think about dying, but I went ahead with my tutorial for Nate and Laura anyway.

To help them understand the importance of protecting their assets, I walked them through a scenario in which they're driving their car through town. When the light turns green, they pull into the intersection, just as we all do a dozen times a day. But in my story, a driver coming the other way is texting and doesn't see his own red light. He flies through the intersection and T-bones Nate and Laura's car.

I asked Nate and Laura to imagine that, as a result of this accident, they walked away, but suffered brain injuries that left them unable to work ever again. "Now what will you do?" I asked.

Nate and Laura talked about the money they each had in savings and some small disability policies they had through their employers. "Will that work?" they asked.

To answer that question, I walked Nate and Laura through some math to put a dollar value on exactly what they would lose if they were never able to work again. What is the financial impact from the permanent loss of a paycheck? Nate was 30 years old and making $100,000 per year. As a rule of thumb to simplify inflation and taxes, we generally say that future income would work out to 20 times the current annual salary. That means that over the course of a lifetime, Nate was looking at $2 million in lost income.

That's a big number, and I let it sink in. Over the years I've seen lots of people pull back and think that's way too high, but Nate thought about it and said, "You know what? I want to protect Laura, so I'm going to get the $2 million life insurance policy. Let's do it."

So I worked up that policy and we made a plan to get together in another six months to start talking about investing. I was thrilled that I had taken my first clients through this process and that they understood what I was telling them and were excited to work with me. It was incredibly validating, and I knew I was on the right path.

Fast forward three months to a hot August day. After an afternoon mowing the lawn, I walked back into the house to find a voicemail from a mutual friend. "Hey, John. I don't know how to tell you this, but Nate died this morning."

To this day, I get a lump in my throat when I think about that voicemail. Nate was only 30. He had his whole life ahead of him, and I thought I would get to walk alongside this fine couple as we moved through life together.

We went through all of the things people go through after a tragedy: the calls, the funeral, the tears. About six weeks later, I met with Laura in my office. I had the proceeds from the life insurance company for her.

We sat in silence, staring at a check for $2 million on the desk between us.

Laura spoke first. "You know," she said quietly, "$2 million isn't really that much money. It's just the money Nate would have made anyway."

And she was right. Nate died, and bam! All of his future income showed up in his checking account at once. The huge amounts of life insurance I had talked about with my mentor in practice exercises—$2 and $3 and $5 million policies—no longer seemed like funny money that couldn't possibly be real. It was all too real, and it represented everything Nate would have given to Laura if he had lived. Because he loved Laura, Nate made sure that he provided for her no matter what: in this case, a lifetime of earnings compressed down into one payment.

UNDERSTANDING HUMAN LIFE VALUE

Nate and Laura's story became a rallying cry for me. I made it my mission to make sure that all of my clients understood exactly what was at stake on the day when they lost their income, whether that was due to retirement, illness, accident, or some tragedy that no one could have predicted.

Make no mistake: you will have to stop working someday. If you're lucky, you'll be able to choose the date. If you're unlucky, your income could stop suddenly, leaving you and your family in a desperate situation where the money runs out long before your life does.

To understand how much money you'll need over the course of your lifetime, it's crucial to calculate what economists call your **Human Life Value**. Human life value is the total income you can expect to earn over the course of your life. This number is the key to planning for the future.

Businesses do this all the time. If you've ever watched Shark Tank, you know that the investors are always asking the contestants what their business valuation is. The ones who get good deals from the Sharks are the ones who can answer that question accurately.

Companies are typically valued by looking at future cash flows. They take their current earnings and project future revenue, then subtract the investments and expenditures they'll make along the way.

Human beings also have cash flows: your paychecks. Generally speaking, your Human Life Value is what you get when you add up all the paychecks you think you will earn in your lifetime, then subtract taxes and the toll inflation will take on your income to get to a present-day lump sum. The actual calculation is a lot more complicated, and actuaries who are way smarter than me will factor in many other variables about your earning potential, life expectancy, and more.

I'm not an actuary by any means, but I still find it useful to use some rough equivalents in my financial planning practice. For Nate and Laura, the Human Life Value number we came up with was $2 million. Yours will be different, but you can figure it out. Just use the calculator below to find your income multiple based on your age, then complete the equation to get a rough estimate of your Human Life Value.

For example, if you're 30 years old and make $200,000 per year, your income multiple is 20. When you multiply your current salary of $200,000 by 20, you get a Human Life Value of $4 million. This is a rough estimate that doesn't account for taxes and inflation, but it also doesn't tally in future raises and promotions. Your ultimate Human Life Value could be more or less, but it's useful to get a number that's in the ballpark.

Go ahead and calculate your own Human Life Value right now:

Your Human Life Value

CURRENT AGE	INCOME MULTIPLE
20 – 40 years	30
41 – 50 years	20
51 – 60 years	15
61 – 65 years	10

$ _____ X _____ = $ _____

Current annual salary   Your income multiple   Human life value[2]

Note: If you're age 66 and above, your human life value is roughly the same as your total net worth because your earning years are largely in the past.

Figure 1: Human Life Value calculator

Your Human Life Value isn't just a handy way to figure out how much life insurance it will take to fully replace lost income if you die during your working years. It's also the foundation for understanding the resources you have for investing, and what type of lifestyle you can reasonably expect.

I once had a client who insisted he wanted to have $10 million by the time he retired. He was 40 years old and made $150,000 per year. Now that you know how to calculate Human Life Value, you can see that if he worked for another 25 years, he could only expect $3.75 million. That number is a long way from $10 million, and it's what he would have if he never spent a penny on *anything*: no food, no clothing, no house.

Obviously, that's not realistic. Most people don't receive their entire Human Life Value in one lump sum. It's stretched over decades, and as you get it, you're using it to live on. You need to make this number last for your whole life—and that takes careful planning.

IT'S ALL ON YOU

Unfortunately, that planning has become harder over the past several decades, thanks to a huge shift in how retirement plans are structured. Up until about 1980 or so, the majority of American workers enjoyed **defined benefit** plans. These are what I call your grandparents' pension. Grandpa went to work every day at the same company for 30 years, and then he got a gold watch and a pension that essentially kept paying him a salary until he died. Defined benefit plans paid out a steady, predictable income throughout retirement, perhaps 80 percent of a preretirement salary after 30 years of work. The formula may vary based on years of service and the generosity of the employer, but this type of retirement plan was typical for everyone from teachers and secretaries to corporate accountants and salesmen.

The beauty of a defined benefit plan was that you always knew exactly how much you would have for retirement, so planning was easy. If you didn't think 80 percent would be enough, you could build a little nest egg on the side to supplement it. You had the ultimate comfort in knowing you could never outlive your pension, and financial planning wasn't really necessary for most Americans—it was already being done for them by their employers.

These lifetime pensions were costly, though, and the pressures of globalization forced corporations to look for ways to get out from under those expensive commitments. Starting in the 1980s, companies began to move away from defined benefit plans, and by 2013 only 34 of the Fortune 500 companies still offered them.[2] Businesses replaced these pensions with **defined contribution** plans. These are the 401(k) plans that are the standard today, in which the worker is the one responsible for saving and investing individually to fund their retirement.

When this shift occurred, the companies softened the blow by promising to match a percentage of the employee's contributions. They agreed to pitch in a little bit, but the reality is that they saved a *lot* of money by not having to fund whole pension plans. They also made the pitch that employees would benefit from the freedom of controlling their own money. Workers could take their 401(k)s with them when they switched jobs, so they wouldn't feel compelled to stay with a

[2] Carlozo, Lou. "Pensions Are Taking the Long, Lonely Road to Retirement." US News and World Report. 20 July 2015. https://money.usnews.com/money/personal-finance/mutual-funds/articles/2015/07/20/pensions-are-taking-the-long-lonely-road-to-retirement.

company for their whole career. They could also choose their own investments and watch their account balance grow, which made them feel wealthy in good economies.

When you do the math, however, the big picture is that moving from defined benefits to defined contributions is a huge challenge for workers. Before, large companies took on the risk of investing, along with all the ups and downs of inflation and actuarial questions about how long their retired workers would live after they stopped working. If you have a 401(k) instead of a pension, that risk is now all on *you*. *You're* the one who has to budget for contributions. *You're* the one who has to make smart investments. And *you're* the one who has to figure out how long you're likely to live when you're done working and how much money you'll need for your future self to thrive.

Once you have a clear picture of your Human Life Value, you have two jobs: protect it and grow it.

Protecting your Human Life Value requires making sure you are insured against four major liabilities:

» **Lawsuits:** We live in a very litigious society, and people sue all the time. If you injure somebody with your car, for example, you could end up on the wrong end of a lawsuit and have a multimillion-dollar problem on your hands.

» **Disability:** If you have an injury or health condition that is serious enough to keep you from working, you could lose a lot of income. Disability benefits from Social Security don't cover much.

» **Poor health:** A chronic health issue that requires expensive medical care—hospitalization, surgeries, drugs—can destroy a budget and eat into your savings quickly.

» **Death:** The premature death of a primary wage earner in your household will endanger the livelihood of everyone else.

This isn't a book about insurance, but making sure you have adequate insurance to cover you for these possibilities is a critical part of any good financial plan. These catastrophes aren't statistically likely to happen to you, but they do happen to someone every day. Protect your family today and your future self tomorrow by keeping your whole Human Life Value in mind as you make insurance decisions. The concept of a lifetime of income is abstract, and the numbers can feel unreal because they seem so big. But your Human Life Value is real, and it's yours. I want you to start to think about your Human Life Value as a tangible asset that you must protect.

Next, you want to find ways to grow your Human Life Value. In the days of your grandfather's pension, workers could find a job with one company and move up the ranks with raises and promotions. Even into the 1980s, you could get some education, build experience, and lock yourself into a job title that you kept until you retired, even if you moved between companies.

Today's employment picture is completely different. I've had many people sit down in my office and announce that they didn't need to worry about building wealth for retirement because they would never stop working. In reality, *56 percent of workers over age 50 lose their jobs* through no fault of their own. Even worse, only *one in ten of those workers is able to find a new job that pays the same* as the one they lost.[3] The loss of income can reverberate for years. Sadly, some people never recover.

So you have to be proactive about making yourself valuable to employers. It's no longer enough to learn a few skills and then ride out the decades until full retirement. With the advent of artificial intelligence and increased automation, many of today's jobs won't exist in a few decades. I encourage all my clients to continue improving and adding skills to their resumes. Maybe you take on different projects or moonlight in another department. Maybe you pick up a side gig or develop a hobby into something more. It's up to you how you stay sharp, but the days of cruising through those last 10 to 15

---

[3] Gosselin, Peter. "If You're Over 50, Chances Are the Decision to Leave a Job Won't be Yours." ProPublica. 28 Dec. 2018. https://www.propublica.org/article/older-workers-united-states-pushed-out-of-work-forced-retirement.

years before retirement are done. You've got to protect your value as a worker just as you would protect any other asset in your life. In doing so, you'll maintain or even grow the grand total of your Human Life Value.

THE LESSON

You will earn a certain amount of money in your life. At some point, the paychecks will permanently stop. Your Human Life Value is finite, and that means your access to money is finite. This is the most important thing to understand about your money, and yet we are conditioned to think that money comes to us every two weeks.

Human beings are creatures of habit, so it's not surprising that we get lulled into a sense of security. After all, we've had decades of training that have shown us that the money we need for the mortgage, groceries, and fun stuff is replenished in our bank account every couple weeks.

But one day, the money will stop, and you will shift to living on your savings. The key to a comfortable retirement is working within your Human Life Value to spread your resources across the course of your *whole* life. To be successful in your financial planning requires a fundamental shift in your thinking: forget the two- or four-week budget period and start thinking about your life as a whole.

When Nate died and left Laura with his entire Human Life Value in one check, it really drove home the concept of Human Life Value for me. Like Nate, you only have a finite amount of money coming your way in your life. The timing of when you receive it will be different, but the math is the same. To care for your loved ones and your future self, you need to treat your Human Life Value like the precious asset it is by protecting and growing it. Do not get lulled into complacency and allow it to slip through your fingers!

Once you figure out your Human Life Value, it's time to figure out how to spread that money across the course of your whole life. How can you make it last? You need to manage your cash flow.

Chapter 4

LIFETIME

CASH FLOW

MANAGEMENT

Ask a typical kid what he wants to be when he grows up, and "pro athlete" is often at the top of the list. That's not surprising, because sports stars are cool, and everyone knows that professional athletes make a ton of money.

Or do they?

The average NFL player has a career that lasts just three and a half years. The average cumulative earning over that career is $6.7 million.[4] On the surface that sounds pretty great, but it's not the whole story.

---

[4] Schwartz, Nick. "The average career earnings of athletes across America's major sports will shock you." USA Today. 24 October 2013. http://ftw.usatoday.com/2013/10/average-career-earnings-nfl-nba-mlb-nhl-mls.

Five years after their playing careers are over, 78 percent of these athletes are completely broke.[5]

Think about that for a moment. A talented kid graduates from college at 22 years old and goes pro. He retires from the league five years later at age 27. By age 32, he declares bankruptcy. That means he spent all of his income, then borrowed money and lost that, too.

It's very, very easy to shake our heads at this, tsk-tsking about how wasteful these kids are. How could they possibly spend millions of dollars like that? We're confident that if *we* were the pro athlete in this story, we would never run out of money. There's no way that would happen to us.

Let's do the math on that. Suppose you went pro at your favorite sport and earned $6 million over your five-year career in your twenties. When you divide that $6 million over your earning years, you've pulled in $1.2 million per year. You're rich!

But what about the rest of your life? You get hurt and can no longer work, the endorsements dry up, and you haven't developed any skills for a career after football. If that $6 million has to last the rest of your life, the calculation is different. When you divide that $6 million

---

[5] Steinberg, Leigh. "5 Reasons Why 80% of Retired NFL Players Go Broke." Forbes. 9 February 2015. http://www.forbes.com/sites/leighsteinberg/2015/02/09/5-reasons-why-80-of-retired -nfl-players-go-broke.

over the 30-year working period that most doctors and lawyers would count on, suddenly you only have $200,000 each year. If you spread it out across a 40-year career, it's only $150,000 annually.

When I tell this story to my clients, they are often shocked to realize that they earn the same over their lifetime as a workaday professional football player. The only difference between you and a journeyman punter is that he got all his money up front, and you're getting yours on the installment plan.

YOUR FINANCIAL LIFE IN THREE ACTS

The problem that athletes often have is that they don't realize—or realize too late—that they need to spread their cash flow over their whole lives. Unfortunately, we all have this problem. Everyone has three phases to their financial life, and to keep the math simple we're going to use a hypothetical 90-year human life span. Obviously, the number of years in each phase will be slightly different for everyone, but for the purposes of this book we're going to break it into 30-year chunks:

» **The First 30:** In your childhood and through college, your financial needs are met. Your parents take care of most of it, and you let them, because you're busy growing, getting an education, and figuring out how to survive on your own.

» **The Middle 30:** From roughly age 30 to age 60, you're working and earning a living. This is your **accumulation phase**, the period of your life in which you will make almost all of the income you've got coming to you. Your Human Life Value is decided here.

» **The Final 30:** Somewhere around age 60, you will stop working, but you could live for another 30 years. This is your **distribution phase**, the period of your life where you'll slowly dole out your savings to cover your living expenses.

The difference between the NFL player and you is that his accumulation phase is short, which leaves him with a very long distribution phase. Sixty years is a long time to live on savings. Would you be able to do it?

For that matter, will you be able to enjoy a similar lifestyle during the Final 30 based on what you saved up during the Middle 30? That's what lifetime cash flow management is all about: making sure that the money you earn in your accumulation phase pays for those years *as well as* the decades in your distribution phase. To put it another way: Each year of income you earn right now has to pay for two years of living—one for your current self and one for your future self.

VISUALIZING YOUR LIFETIME
CASH FLOW

Because your lifetime income doesn't come in a lump sum, you need a clear vision of your biggest earning years as well as all the ways that events can conspire to eat away at your wealth to find balance and achieve your goals. For most people, it's easy to track how money flows in every two weeks and flows out as you pay your bills. It's much harder to zoom out to the big picture of lifetime cash flow.

So let's break it down step by step.

This is you, and this is the timeline of your working and retirement life:

Timeline of Your Working and Retirement Life
(Middle 30 and Final 30)

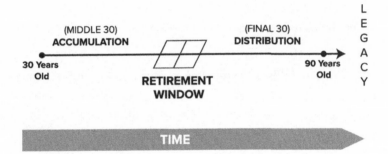

Figure 2: Hypothetical example for illustrative purposes only.

The first decades of your life are paid for by your parents, but eventually you become an adult and you're on your own. You're now in the accumulation phase of your life and making money. From that point, you *could* work straight through your life until you die of old age. But if you wanted to do that, you probably wouldn't be reading this book. Instead, you're looking to enjoy a window of retirement somewhere along the way. You may not know exactly when it will happen or how long it will last, but you definitely want it to be there. Once you retire, you enter the distribution phase, where you live off your savings and investments.

Nobody knows their exact life expectancy, but you may have a number in mind for yourself based on family history, your health, and your tendency to be an optimist or a pessimist. Given the reality of medical advancements, though, I always encourage my clients to bet on living to be 100. It happens more often than you think, and you don't want to outlive your money.

In fact, you may even want to have money left over after you die so you can take care of the loved ones you leave behind. This is the legacy phase of your financial life, in which money is passed on to your heirs.

There's one thing that I know for sure about you, even though we've never met: as long as you're alive, you're going to need money. And the older you get, the more of it you're going to need to fund your lifestyle:

Timeline of Your Working and Retirement Life
(Middle 30 and Final 30)

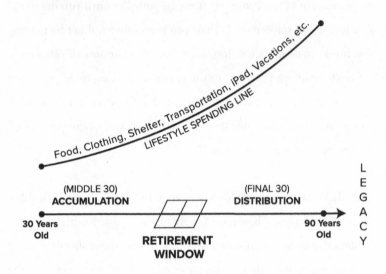

LIFESTYLE SPENDING LINE — Always increasing due to inflation, new inventions, planned obsolescence, marginal propensity to consume, etc.

TIME

Figure 3: Hypothetical example for illustrative purposes only.

When you first start working, you're mostly concerned with covering your basic needs: food, shelter, and clothing. As you start earning a little more, you're able to enhance your lifestyle with extras like vacations, electronics, and maybe some nice furniture. Eventually you might also be paying for your own kids' first 30 years of life, meeting their needs and wants on top of your own.

The list of things you can spend on is endless, and eventually you'll run out of room on your lifestyle line to cover them all. Our needs and wants are unlimited. In fact, there are things that haven't even been invented yet that will fill your list, just like smartphones went from being a twinkle in Steve Jobs' eye to a necessity over the past 15 years. Inflation also pushes prices up, so this line of lifestyle spending will always be increasing over the course of your life.

You're not only spending your way through life though. You're also earning money and building your wealth. Ideally, you're creating a money mountain that grows throughout your earning years:

Timeline of Your Working and Retirement Life
(Middle 30 and Final 30)

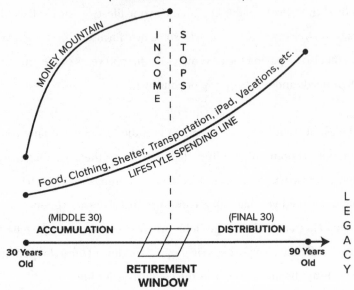

INCOME STOPS LINE — Permanent loss of paycheck and transition to reliance on your MONEY MOUNTAIN

TIME

Figure 4: Hypothetical example for illustrative purposes only.

Your money mountain grows until one day you're worth the most you're ever going to be worth in your life. That's the day before you retire, because the retirement marks the shift from your accumulation phase to your distribution phase.

The day you retire, your income stops. Forever. This is the day that your biweekly stream of paychecks stops and you start paying yourself. From here on out, you need to rely on your money mountain to replace those paychecks, and that means your money mountain is shrinking.

In a perfect world, your money mountain runs out on the day you and your spouse die simultaneously in your sleep. Your net worth is perfectly distributed in a steady, even cash flow for exactly as long as you need it:

Timeline of Your Working and Retirement Life
(Middle 30 and Final 30)

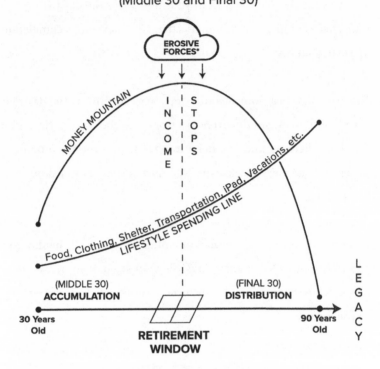

*EROSIVE FORCES: Market Risk, Interest Rate Risk, Inflation, Legislative Risk, Longevity, Personal Lawsuit, Sickness, Death

TIME

Figure 5: Hypothetical example for illustrative purposes only.

This is what's supposed to happen, but it only works if you manage your cash flow so that your money mountain of savings lasts. This is a challenge, especially in the face of lifestyle spending that just keeps going up. Your money mountain has to be big enough to maintain your lifestyle.

What happens if your lifestyle spending line is too high? It eats away at your money mountain faster, and you run out of cash:

Timeline of Your Working and Retirement Life
(Middle 30 and Final 30)

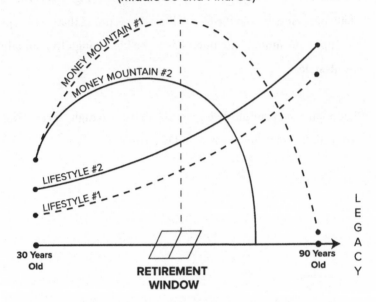

LIFESTYLE #1 and MONEY MOUNTAIN #1 — **SUSTAINABLE**

LIFESTYLE #2 leads to full depletion of MONEY MOUNTAIN #2—
OUTLIVE MONEY

Figure 6: Hypothetical example for illustrative purposes only.

When your mountain of wealth isn't sufficient to meet your lifestyle needs, you have two choices: move your retirement window to a later date or hope you die sooner. These aren't great options, but that's reality. *Your money mountain is finite.*

Now is a good time to mention that most people aren't entirely honest with themselves when they sit down to determine that ever-increasing line of spending. When asked, people typically estimate that they will need 70 to 80 percent of their preretirement income during retirement. But when researchers asked people to describe how they wanted to spend their time in retirement and assigned reasonable cost estimates to those activities, they found that the percentage of preretirement income required to live the dream was more like *130 percent*.[6]

Finally, there are also economic forces that threaten to erode your money mountain even as you're working to build it up. These forces include:

» **Market risk:** A significant economic downturn before or during retirement.

---

[6] Ariely, Dan and Aline Holzwarth. "How Much Money Will You Really Spend in Retirement? Probably a Lot More Than You Think." Wall Street Journal. 3 September 2018. https://www.wsj.com/articles/how-much-money-will-you-really-spend-in-retirement-probably-a-lot-more-than-you-think-1536026820.

» **Interest rate risk:** Rates drop and/or remain low during retirement.

» **Inflation risk:** Inflation rises and you lose purchasing power.

» **Legislative risk:** Taxes go up during retirement.

» **Longevity risk:** You and/or your spouse outlive your money.

» **Personal lawsuits:** You are successfully sued for damages.

» **Sickness and accidents:** You permanently lose the ability to work.

» **Premature death:** You or your spouse suffers a permanent loss of income.

All of these forces are largely out of your control, but a good financial plan will account for them and work to minimize your exposure to these risks. Thanks to the media, most people are focused solely on the rate of return on their 401(k) as a measure of success, but financial planning doesn't start and stop with that. It mitigates threats and focuses on creating dependable cash flow that will last throughout your entire distribution phase. A solid financial plan is about lifetime cash flow, not just tracking the stock market.

THE LESSON

The single most important thing to understand about lifetime cash flow is this: the money you earn during the Middle 30 is what you have available to fund the last 60 years—or more!—of your life. What you earn now must cover your lifestyle expenses during both the Middle 30 and the Final 30. That's a big burden on your prime earning years, and you need to clearly see how the money flows across your lifetime in order to plan for your retirement.

Everyone loves to judge the athlete who goes broke, but the reality is that we're all that guy. Every one of us has a finite amount of lifetime earnings that we need to make last for our whole lives. The only difference is that an athlete going broke is a sensational news story, but we never read about the doctor who goes broke at age 70 because it happens in slow motion, taking decades rather than a few years.

So how do you manage your lifetime cash flow so that you don't end up robbing your future self of a good life? The One-Number Budget makes it easy.

Chapter 5

THE ONE-NUMBER
BUDGET

Remember Mike and Lauren, the clients I took to lunch in a fit of frustration? No matter how many times I went over an old-fashioned budget with them, I could never get them to commit to putting more of their money into wealth building, even though they had plenty to spare.

Back when I was still trying to use a traditional budget, this is what we would be looking at:

Cash Flow Visibility Worksheet
Prepared for Mike & Lauren

EXPENSES		INCOME	
Grocery	$450	Mike Salary	$80,000
Dining Out	$450	Mike Bonus	$10,000
Non-Grocery (Target)	$350	Lauren Salary	$90,000
Auto Fuel	$125	Lauren Bonus	$20,000
Auto Maintenance	$150	Rental/Other	$0
Wireless Phone	$45		
Parking/Tolls	$50	**Total Income**	**$200,000**
Clothing & Dry Cleaning	$100	6.0% to 401(k)/403(b)	$12,000
Vacation	$200		
Medical/Personal Maint.	$250	**Estimated Net after Tax Cash Flow**	
Debt Payments (Student Loan)	$500	Gross Inc. - Retirement	$188,000
		Less Taxes 30.0%	($56,400)
Protection (Liab, D/L, Life, etc.)	$450		
Utilities	$250	**Net after Tax Income**	
Phone, Cable, Internet	$250	Annual	$131,600
Household (Security, Maid)	$300	Monthly	$10,967
		Weekly	$2,531
Mortgage (P/L, Taxes, etc.)	$2,500		
Auto Payments	$500		
Childcare	$1,500		
Child Support	$0		
Alimony	$0		
Charity	$250		

Total Monthly Expenses $8,670

Total Monthly Income:	$10,967
Total Monthly Expenses:	$8,670
Estimated Monthly Surplus	**$2,297**

Figure 7: Cash flow visibility worksheet example

As we discussed in Chapter 2, this is way too complicated, and it was too much work for Mike and Lauren to update the numbers regularly. After all that work, I wanted them to focus on their monthly surplus, which you and I can see is a pretty big number.

I tried every way I could think of to convince them to channel that surplus into wealth building, but in the end, Mike and Lauren didn't see the surplus as a big number. The minute we began discussing an automatic savings plan or redirecting the extra cash into their 401(k)s, they began to sing.

"We-ell...I don't kno-ow..." And this melodic phrase always led to them negotiating their number down to just a fraction of the surplus. They just couldn't commit.

It finally dawned on me that Mike and Lauren never felt like they had extra money. Instead, they felt like I was trying to take it away from them, and their decisions were a knee-jerk reaction to perceived scarcity.

This is a tricky bit of psychology. First, because traditional budgets are never perfect, Mike and Lauren were worried that they might not actually have $2,200 at the end of each month. What about the leaky roof or cat's hip replacement? They were afraid to lose the money they'd been using for unexpected bills, so they felt like their money was scarce when they actually had plenty to work with.

They were also reluctant to give up control of that money. Instead of committing to systematic savings, they wanted to be able to make choices each month. It's nice to have $500 extra for a weekend trip or lacrosse camp for the kids. They may have had good intentions about choosing to put at least some of the surplus into savings, but it never happened. As we discussed in Chapter 1, stealing from your future self feels like a victimless crime. It's painless today to lose your surplus to other priorities, but eventually it catches up with you.

With the traditional budget, the surplus was the last number Mike and Lauren saw, so it felt like their last chance to hang on to their hard-earned money. I knew we had to turn that thinking upside-down.

THE ONE-NUMBER BUDGET, STEP BY STEP

Now that you understand the big picture of lifetime cash flow management, you know how important it is to make sure your income right now pays not just for today but for tomorrow as well. Remember, your earnings during the middle third of your life have to cover your living expenses for those years *and* for the final third of your life. One day those paychecks will stop, and you need to be ready.

So how do you make that happen?

The answer is the One-Number Budget. Here's how it works.

The One-Number Budget

Gross Household Income (annual):		$_____	
Wealth Building for Retirement = 20%	X .20	= $_____	
Taxes (Federal, State, Local, Real Estate) = 30%	X .30	= $_____	
Lifestyle Expenses = 45%	X .45	= $_____	
Total Monthly Lifestyle Expenses	÷ 12 = $_____		
Less Housing: (15% of gross income ÷ 12)	– $_____		
Less Other Fixed Expenses (student loans, etc.)	– $_____		
Your One-Number Budget for the Month:	Total: $_____		

Figure 8: The One-Number Budget

To better understand how it works, let's walk through the numbers with our friends Mike and Lauren. Here's what Mike and Lauren's One-Number Budget looks like, based on their income and expenses:

Mike and Lauren's One-Number Budget

Gross Household Income (annual):	$200,000	
Wealth Building for Retirement = 20%	X .20	= $40,000
Taxes (Federal, State, Local, Real Estate) = 30%	X .30	= $60,000
Lifestyle Expenses = 50%	X .50	= $100,000
Total Monthly Lifestyle Expenses	÷ 12 = $8,333	
Less Housing: (15% of $200,000 ÷ 12)	− $2,500	
Less Other Fixed Expenses (student loans, etc.)	− $500	
Mike & Lauren's One-Number Budget for the Month:	**Total: $5,333**	

Note: The above calculations and percentages are for illustrative purposes only and are not deemed to be used as tax advice. For tax advice specific to your situation, please contact a CPA or tax attorney for help.

Figure 9: One-Number Budget example

Mike and Lauren's total household income is $200,000 each year, which includes both his salary and her online business income. Knowing exactly what you have coming in is the first step, and many people aren't exactly sure. If you have direct deposit and haven't actually looked at a pay stub in a while, take the time to review your monthly income with your paychecks or your annual income from last year that you reported on your tax return. This is what you have to work with, and you need the number in your head—and on paper.

You'll notice that the very first line item on the One-Number Budget is your retirement savings. When I talk about wealth building, that's the money that needs to get you through the final third of your life. The very first thing I want you to do with your money is be selfish with it: take 20 percent of your gross income and save it for the future. You *will* have to stop working at some point, whether by choice or by life intervening. I don't know if your employer has told you this yet, but when you stop showing up, they stop paying you. You have to get ready to pay yourself.

I've been advising people for a long time, and over the years I've learned that if you consistently save 20 percent of your income over a period of 20 to 30 years, you put yourself in the best position to avoid money problems. If you're starting your savings plan later in life, you may need to be even more aggressive—but 20 percent is a good place to start. In Mike's case, he'll be saving $40,000 each year in a combination of investments for both him and his wife.

Next, we budget for taxes. You may have noticed that the IRS will collect their share every year no matter what you do, so this is a nonnegotiable line item. Note that the 30 percent figure I use in the One-Number Budget is to create a useful cash flow simulation, but it's not perfect. This is a broad figure that combines federal, state, local, and real estate taxes into a rough estimate that's about right for the majority of my clients. Your numbers will vary based on your own circumstances, so if you're interested in drilling down to an exact percentage here, you should consult a tax professional.

So Mike subtracts $60,000 off the top for the tax man. Since he automatically pays his property taxes through his mortgage lender and his federal and state income taxes are covered by withholding, he's surprised by this number. You might be, too—it's probably the first time you've thought about your tax burden as a lump sum.

What's left over for living? About half of your gross income. In Mike and Lauren's case, that's $100,000. At this point, it makes sense to break that big amount down to cover monthly expenses, since that's how most bills arrive, and it's how we've been trained to think about our cash. For Mike and Lauren, that means $8,333 to spend on everything they need for the month.

We're not quite down to Mike and Lauren's One Number yet though. There are some big living expenses that it makes sense to take out of the equation first. That's because these are fixed expenses that you absolutely have to pay every month. Your housing costs (mortgage or rent) are the biggest, so that comes first.

You'll notice that in the One-Number Budget I recommend you spend no more than 15 percent of your income on housing. Why? Because limiting this expense makes it much easier to save 20 percent of your income and still enjoy your life right now. I get a lot of pushback on this from people who live in expensive housing markets. I live in the DC area, so believe me, I get it. My experience working with clients has shown me time and again that if your housing costs are much more than 15 percent of your total income, you'll struggle to meet your savings goals. Stick with me for now—we'll talk more about how to work within this number in Chapter 6.

Next, we have a line item for other fixed monthly expenses. The two most common are student loans and childcare, especially for young professionals. You might also have other fixed expenses, but you don't have to get too far into the weeds here. The point is to subtract the nonnegotiables so you have a better picture of what's left for life-style expenses.

Subtract those big-ticket items, and you are left with your One Number. This is the amount you have for everything else in your life.

Can you live on your One Number? Can you get through four weeks on that amount?

For Mike and Lauren, the answer was yes. A grand total of $5,333 to spend felt completely doable to them. In fact, they finally felt like they had plenty of money to spend exactly as they wanted. We eliminated their scarcity mindset and replaced it with a number that they could feel good about every month. They never complained about saving 20 percent of their income again, because it was *already taken care of.*

WHY IT WORKS

The beauty of the One-Number Budget is that it streamlines the budgeting process: no more sorting through endless line items to figure out how much you have left over. All you have to do is manage your spending to *one number*.

Your One Number covers everything you need to live—and I do mean everything. I'm talking about:

» Electricity and other utilities

» Food

» Clothing

» Cars

» Vacations

» Electronics

» Credit card debt

» College tuition

» Hobbies

And anything else you want or need. Instead of worrying about every little receipt, you just have to make sure your total monthly spending falls within your One Number. That's it. If you can do that, everything else automatically works, and your wealth building for retirement is taken care of.

There are several ways to streamline your finances to stay within your One Number each month. I recommend setting up one checking account that you use for your lifestyle expenses. You can direct deposit or automatically transfer the full monthly amount of your One Number into this account, then use it to pay the bills and expenses as they come. You do have to watch your balance to make sure you don't overdraw near the end of the month, but modern technology makes that pretty easy. You may even be able to set up an alert to let you know when you're getting close.

I have clients who love their air miles credit cards, and they put all their lifestyle expenses on that card. When they hit their One Number limit, it's time to stop. This is only a good solution if you are religious about paying the balance in full every month though—it may not work for everyone.

Once you create a system for sticking to your One Number, you enjoy the benefits of enhanced decision-making. For example, if you're shopping for your dream car and find out that it will take a $1,000 monthly payment to afford it, you can easily check that amount against your One Number. Will you have enough left for everything else? Are you happy to manage your other expenses so that $1,000 fits into your plan? If you're a major gearhead and you are willing to eat ramen to do it, go for it! My job as a financial advisor has never been to play Big Brother and tell you how to spend your money. That's all up to you. The One-Number Budget gives you the clarity to see how your spending choices will affect the rest of your lifestyle so you can make decisions that work for you.

These decisions will also work for your future self, because the One-Number Budget puts wealth building *first*. Notice that the very first thing we do with the One-Number Budget is allocate 20 percent of your income for savings. That's automatic, and it ensures that your future self is always represented in your decision-making. Because this money never makes it into your checking account, you won't even miss it.

Human beings are incredibly adaptable creatures. We've figured out how to live in the desert and in Antarctica. We can adjust our diets to fit what's available in hundreds of cultures and ecosystems. And we can get used to changes in our budgets, too. You've probably already experienced this phenomenon when you've gotten a raise. It feels like a lot of money at first, but pretty soon you adapt to your new circumstances and your lifestyle spending increases to absorb the difference.

The One-Number Budget helps you do the opposite. Instead of basing your lifestyle spending choices on keeping up with the Joneses—or these days, maybe the Kardashians—you instead make your decisions based on your One Number. This is what you can really afford while ensuring that your future self enjoys the same quality of life you have today.

PROGRESS, NOT PERFECTION

When Mike and Lauren saw their One Number, they realized they could easily live within it. Can you live within yours?

If you can't, I don't want you to give up. As Dan Sullivan of Strategic Coach® is famous for saying, we're focused on progress, not perfection. Traditional budgets make you feel bad about yourself so you want to quit, but the One-Number Budget is designed to help you get on the path to success.

I work with many clients who have begun to save for their retirement, but they know they should be doing more. A typical scenario would be one in which a couple earning $200,000 per year had maxed out one spouse's 401(k) at $19,500 per year. That's a lot of money!

But to maintain their lifestyle, it won't be enough. Right now that couple has achieved a savings rate of 9.75 percent. That's better than the average American's personal savings rate, which hovered around 7.6 percent between 1980 and 2021.[7] Still, they'll want to work toward the 20 percent goal.

That might not happen overnight, but it often happens faster than you expect. Each time you get a raise or a promotion, you can allocate that extra to your wealth building, which will painlessly boost your savings percentage. You can also shift just some of your One Number to savings and gradually adjust your lifestyle to your new number. You don't have to solve this by Friday. It's okay to take some time to build up to the 20 percent goal.

What I often see is that, once my clients understand the gap between their target savings rate and their actual savings rate, they start to get competitive with themselves. It becomes a game: how fast can we get to 20 percent? You might surprise yourself.

THE LESSON

Simplicity is key to taking action, and *action is key to getting results.*

---

[7] Federal Reserve Economic Data (FRED). https://fred.stlouisfed.org/series/psavert.

The One-Number Budget works because it's easy to understand and stick with. By putting savings first, it gives your future self a seat at the table and prevents you from becoming the thief that robs you of a good retirement. When you drill down to your One Number, you know exactly what you have to work with, so you can make lifestyle decisions accordingly. No more flying blind and hoping for the best. With the One-Number Budget, you know exactly what you have to work with to live your best life, both today and in the future.

The One-Number Budget has transformed my work with clients. I have seen firsthand how they become empowered not just to understand their cash flow, but to take positive actions that set them up for future success.

It's also just so *easy*. Within 30 seconds we can update their cash flow worksheet during our annual review. I add up their new income, and we check to see if their savings matches. If it doesn't, we adjust their 401(k) contributions or capture that wealth in other investment vehicles. That's it.

My sincere hope is that the One-Number Budget offers you this life-changing simplicity and clarity, too. Try it. If you find that a 20 percent savings rate is out of reach right now, it's okay to work up to it. With a clear view of your finances, you'll find it much easier to get where you're going.

Calculating your One Number is only the first step though. You also need to learn to live within it.

Chapter 6

HOW TO WORK
WITH YOUR
NUMBER

I hated school when I was younger. I was never a great student, and I didn't want to be there. After a year of actively trying to be invisible at my high school, at the start of my sophomore year I decided to do something different. I wanted to have more fun, and I wanted my dad to be proud of me.

So I started weightlifting.

I went to a relatively small school in New York, but I didn't know anybody who was going out for weightlifting. I just showed up. I didn't know what I was doing, and there wasn't a lot of guidance. The teacher in charge was a good guy, but he taught seniors so I didn't know him well. His job in the weight room was just to supervise, not to coach, so he basically opened the door and let everyone do their own thing.

Just inside the door to the weight room was a big power bench, and there were two guys there banging away at that thing all the time. I had to walk past them to get to the other equipment, and I was a little in awe of them. They were upperclassmen, and they were cool.

Eventually these guys, Ed and Marshall, took pity on me. I'm sure they could tell I was kind of lost, and they asked me if I wanted to work out with them. They took me under their wing, and suddenly school felt a whole lot more fun.

Ed and Marshall were also on the track team, and they were always talking about how awesome it was. They talked about winter track all the time, and soon they were including me in those statements, saying things about *when* I joined track instead of *if*.

The fact that these cool upperclassmen would talk to me at all blew my mind. I didn't think running sounded like much fun—let alone running in the cold—but I also knew that if I wanted to continue to hang out with these guys, I needed to be where they were.

So I joined the track team.

What I didn't know was that our school track team was a perennial county champion. We were stacked with runners who held multiple titles across different events.

I was not that athletic, and all I wanted to do was hang out with Ed and Marshall. I couldn't keep up with them because I wasn't very fast. Every day I hurt, from my legs to my lungs.

One day during an exceptionally difficult workout, Coach was at the far end of the track, calling out times as the runners passed him. Instead of staying with the pack and rounding the far turn to hear my time, I just kept running straight for the fence around the perimeter of the track. I was gasping for breath and my lungs were on fire. I held on to that chain link like it was the only thing between me and total collapse.

Panting, I thought to myself, "This is nuts. Coach is just going to have to give me something else to do." I stood there having a pity party for one while the rest of my teammates rounded the oval and headed back in my direction. I started to stretch out an imaginary hamstring injury to cover for my weakness. I didn't want anyone to know I gave up.

In the middle of my pseudo-stretching, I peeked under my arm at the guys coming around the track to see if anyone was looking at me. They weren't. Each runner's face was red from the cold and exertion. They frowned in concentration. I could see they were also in pain.

But they were still running.

That's when it hit me: there are no special workouts.

If I wanted to be like those champion runners, I had to do what they were doing. I couldn't ask the coach for a special workout, because it wouldn't get me where I wanted to go.

When the team came around the oval again, I peeled myself off of the fence and rejoined practice. "No special workouts," I muttered to myself. I kept running, day after day and month after month. I didn't always want to, but I kept at it.

I lost a lot of races that year, many by spectacular margins, and I often wanted to quit. But by the end of the spring track season, Coach put me on the relay at the championship meet. I was shocked that I got the spot, and it was an incredible honor after my very weak start on the track team. We came in second, which meant an All-League Honorable Mention. Now I had a title, just like my teammates. I had accomplished something that I never dreamed of doing before, and it changed my entire outlook on what was possible.

This was a lightbulb moment for me, and it's stuck with me my whole life. *There are no special workouts.* Whether you want to run faster or save money for the future, you have to do the work.

NO SPECIAL WORKOUTS

As a high school athlete, I was fortunate to work with a great coach who laid out a path for success and held me accountable for doing the work I needed to do to get there. As an adult, I realize just how valuable this experience was, and I want nothing more than to provide you with that same type of guidance. Consider me your financial coach: I want you to push the boundaries of what you thought was possible and get on track for financial success.

But I can only serve as your guide. I can't run the race for you, and I can't do the work for you—though I'll definitely be cheering you on! Only *you* can do the work that it takes to put your finances in order and save for a comfortable retirement.

In my work, I often meet with clients who are essentially asking me to come up with a special workout for their financial plan. When I finish explaining how a 20 percent savings rate will empower them to live the life they want, they nod quietly.

Then they ask for a special workout.

"I get where you're coming from," they say, "but housing is really expensive where I live. Can I spend 20 percent on housing and save 15 percent instead?"

Here's the thing. Your retirement doesn't care about today's housing costs. You either have an asset that's going to recreate your income during retirement, or you don't. Asking for an exception to the 20 percent savings rate is like going into the grocery store and telling the cashier that you'd like a discount on your bill because housing is too expensive right now.

That's just not how it works.

The same was true for my track meets. None of the other athletes or officials cared about how much I hated running in the snow. If I didn't do the workout, I wouldn't have been ready. If you don't do the work with your budget, you won't be ready to retire.

It's as simple as that. This isn't easy to hear, but no good coach is going to sugarcoat the truth for you. Instead, they're going to give you the tools you need to succeed. Once you've committed to the work, the tools will change your life.

And that's what I want for you: to give you exactly what you need to change your financial life.

The One-Number Budget works. You just have to work within it.

LIVING YOUR LIFE INSIDE
ONE NUMBER

If you filled out your One-Number Budget in the previous chapter and were surprised at what you saw, you're definitely not alone. I've worked with many clients over the years who look at the numbers and need to sit with them for a moment to let them sink in.

Some people have to own up to the fact that they're currently only saving 5 or 7 percent of their gross income for retirement. Others are faced with the reality that they are overspending on housing, and they're not sure what to do. Still others have large student loan payments that cut into their One Number for living.

Deep breaths. Remember, we're after progress, not perfection. If you're sitting at a 5 percent savings rate and 20 percent looks completely impossible, I don't want you to panic. You might not be able to hit 20 percent this year or next, but you can't let that stop you from moving toward that goal. So how can you gain some momentum to build your savings rate over time?

First, start at the top line, which is your savings rate. Can you increase your contribution to your 401(k) by 1 to 2 percent this year? Most people won't notice a small increase and can easily adjust to that type of change in their One Number for living expenses.

This, by the way, is exactly the same strategy that the federal government uses to collect taxes. Uncle Sam withholds your taxes right off the top, so you never even realize you earned this money. The government makes sure it gets paid first, and you automatically adjust your standard of living to what's left over when you cash your check.

You can do this for yourself by fine-tuning the amount you put toward savings right off the top. Schedule an additional 1 to 3 percent to go directly into your retirement plan either through paycheck withholding or an automatic savings plan. Try it for a month and see how you feel. Most people naturally adjust to their new normal and find the increased savings painless. It's easy to dial your savings up a tick or two at a time, and eventually you'll reach your goal.

Next, make a plan to allocate your next few raises to your savings instead of absorbing them into your budget without thinking about it. Each time you get a promotion or a raise, you should recalculate your One-Number Budget to reflect your new income. First, celebrate by adding some of this money to your One Number for lifestyle spending—you've earned it, and you should enjoy it! But you should also allocate a good portion of that new income toward getting your savings rate up.

When you first get your raise, you're not addicted to that money yet. It's the perfect moment to boost your savings rate, because your lifestyle doesn't have to change at all to accommodate the shift. If you're feeling a scarcity mindset nagging at you and trying to convince you that you don't have enough to spend, remind yourself of this: as soon as you get your savings rate to 20 percent, everything is easy. Once you're at 20 percent, your next raise requires just a minor tweak and you can enjoy the rest. And you'll feel a whole lot better celebrating that promotion knowing you've taken care of your future self.

Another area where you may be able to find money to redirect into wealth-building is with your credit card debt. If you're carrying a balance of $25,000 per year and your card has a typical interest rate of 15 percent, that's $3,750 per year just disappearing into thin air as you make your payments. If you can knock out your debt, you'll recapture cash flow that's going toward interest and be able to put it directly into your savings, which will get you even closer to that 20 percent goal. Debt is a trap that gives you the illusion of control, but in reality it takes away your choices. It makes you think you can spend now and pay later, but it's actually a pipeline that siphons money away from your future self. Getting rid of your consumer debt—credit cards, car loans, student loans—is a major key to financial health, and we'll talk more about it in Chapter 7.

Is putting your raise toward your savings the most fun thing you can do? Nope. Is paying down your credit debt exciting? Not for most people. But I guarantee you that as you watch your savings rate grow, you'll be more motivated. I've seen this time and again with clients who thought they could never do it, but the closer they get, the more excited they are. And then they're suddenly finding more ways to boost their savings, whether it's by trimming spending here and there or making bigger lifestyle changes.

I know you probably have more questions about the best way to cut your spending and build your savings rate. Maybe you picked up this book hoping I would tell you exactly how many times you can eat out this week and still have enough money to retire.

Most budget books are prescriptive, telling you what you should and shouldn't spend your money on. Most financial gurus will command you not to buy coffee on your way to work while wagging a finger at you disapprovingly. Whether they say it out loud or not, they're calling you and your choices stupid.

I don't do that.

Telling you how to spend your money is the same as telling you how to live your life. But you and I are completely different people, with different values and goals. You should build your life around *your* values. If you try to build it around mine, your budget is doomed to fail, and you'll end up right back at square one.

Your One Number is your North Star. If you're someone who loves cars but doesn't need a mansion to be happy, you can divvy up your living expenses within your One Number to reflect that. If you want to eat out every night, go for it.

The One Number tells you how much money is available, but it's up to *you* to set priorities and make spending decisions.

After you reach your 20 percent savings goal, you can spend all of your One Number. Spend it any way that you want. Just don't spend more than what the One Number says you have available.

ENHANCED DECISION-MAKING

One of the reasons that the One-Number Budget is so successful is because it streamlines your financial decision-making. It makes absolutely clear what you have left for discretionary spending—the lifestyle expenses that you attend to after you take your wealth building and tax obligations off the top.

The One-Number Budget is simple, but it's not necessarily easy. Just like winning a track championship, it takes plenty of work to stick to your plan and make your savings a priority. In order to make it work, sometimes you'll have to make hard choices.

And that brings us to my recommendation about housing costs. I firmly believe that, for most people, keeping your housing costs—the amount you spend on rent or your mortgage—to 15 percent of your gross income is the key to future wealth. I've worked with many clients over the years, and most of the ones who go on to comfortable retirements are the ones who keep their housing costs at or below 15 percent of their gross income—and push the balance into their 20 percent savings rate.

Part of the problem is that, sure, the cost of living is quite high in many areas of the country, particularly large cities on the coasts. You don't have to convince me of this—I live in the DC Metro area, one of the most expensive housing markets in the country! But you still have choices.

One of the reasons people feel trapped by housing costs is that they base their housing budget on the maximum amount mortgage companies or big banks will lend them, rather than on what they can actually afford to spend. The mortgage company doesn't know your budget or your goals. They only know that they want to make a profit, and they base their lending amounts on the highest possible amount they think you can pay back without risking default. That mindset typically leads to numbers that assume you love eating ramen and don't want any furniture in your new place.

They're also not taking into account any of your other personal goals. For example, if you are buying the house because you're planning to start a family, you'll need to consider the cost of childcare and all of the many expenses that you'll be faced with for the next couple decades as you raise a baby into a self-sufficient human.

When it comes to working with your One Number, you need to be realistic about those fixed expenses. If you go beyond 15 percent on your housing, you simply won't have much left for the rest of your lifestyle, and you'll need to make choices. Will you have a car? Skip vacations? Have one child instead of three? It's all up to you. While the One-Number Budget can't make decisions for you, it will also never lie to you. Instead, you get an honest look at what you have to spend on your lifestyle while still looking out for your future self.

When it comes to housing, you do have another option: move. That may sound unreasonable, but I want you to remember that you have options. If you can move to a city where housing costs are more reasonable, then in some instances you can take a lower salary but still come out financially stronger. I've had clients crunch the numbers and discover that this was their best shot at getting to that 20 percent savings rate without changing a single thing about the rest of their lifestyle. I'm not saying this is the best choice for everyone, but it is a choice.

And that's what the One-Number Budget does. It brings into sharp focus the resources you have, so you can make decisions based on the lifestyle you can afford. And if you really can't live with those choices, then you know that you need to change course to earn more money or find a place where the things you want cost less. It requires focus to stick to your numbers, but that effort *will* get you the results your future self is counting on.

THE BENEFITS OF A
20 PERCENT SAVINGS RATE

If you haven't yet reached your 20 percent savings rate, I want to convince you to keep working toward that goal. Saving 20 percent puts you in the best position to have enough money to maintain your current lifestyle throughout your retirement years. When those paychecks finally stop coming, your money mountain will be high enough to get you through the rest of your life.

A 20 percent savings rate also allows you some flexibility to weather financial storms right now. If your income takes a temporary hit—as happened to so many people during the pandemic—you can easily dial back your savings for a bit as you ride out a short-term period of lost income.

For example, I worked with a couple who did everything I recommended and followed the One-Number Budget to the letter. When the Great Recession hit back in 2008, they were both working for the same company. That company cut salaries by 10 percent across the board, with a promise to restore them once conditions improved.

When we sat down together to review what that drop in income meant for them, I saw that they had built up a sizable cash reserve. My only recommendation was to dial back their 401(k) contributions a bit, but otherwise they could go on as if nothing had happened. They were floored.

In the end, they opted to cut some discretionary spending instead of reducing their savings rate, but they were able to make that decision with open eyes. Because they had saved so diligently, they had four tools at their disposal to deal with the economic downturn:

» Reduce expenses

» *Temporarily* dial back savings

» Use cash reserves

» A combination of any of the above

Because they were in the habit of saving 20 percent of their gross income, they were in a position of strength to deal with a temporary disruption in their cash flow. Once conditions improved, their employer restored their salaries and they went back to following their original One-Number Budget.

When you save 20 percent of your income, you're also artificially living below your capacity. You've already adjusted your lifestyle spending to be well under your income, so you're not living paycheck to paycheck. This gives you flexibility during a short-term period of strain, and it also sets you up for success once you're retired. That's because you only need to replace 80 percent of your preretirement income to feel good about your lifestyle. You're already there. Replacing just 80 percent of your income is obviously easier than replacing 100 percent, so that green mountain of wealth will last you longer—all without you having to sacrifice things you enjoy once you retire.

THE LESSON

Writer and former Yahoo executive Tim Sanders has a saying that really resonates with me: "Education without application is just entertainment."

And it's true. It's not enough just to read about your finances or losing weight or winning a race. You have to be willing to put in the work to get the job done. The One-Number Budget is here to help you zero in on the changes that will put you on the path to an enjoyable retirement:

» Pay yourself first by saving 20 percent of your gross income.

» Increase your income while keeping your discretionary spending flat.

» Experiment with your numbers to combat a scarcity mindset.

This is how you work with your One Number. Start by making your savings automatic right off the top of your budget, so you don't miss it. If you need to build up to your 20 percent goal, that's fine—just be sure to allocate a good portion of your raises and bonuses to savings while you continue spending as you always have. This takes "keeping up with the Joneses" off the table and lets you focus on living within *your* means. It also keeps you from mindlessly adapting to an increasing income by spending it all.

Finally, I encourage you to revisit your savings rate regularly and try dialing up your savings bit by bit. When you use a slow and steady hand to build your automatic savings, you will never feel deprived by minute changes in your One Number. You'll automatically adjust, and you'll probably even find yourself encouraged to do even more. Treat it like a little competition with yourself, and you'll get to the finish line faster than you thought possible.

The forces of economics move without our input, and there's a lot out there that you simply cannot control. You can't count on the stock market to bail you out if you keep stealing a little here and there from your future self. You can't control future tax increases. The thing you can control is your saving and spending.

In money as in life, there are no special workouts. There's no money hack that's going to let you retire like Elon Musk with only a 5 percent saving rate. It simply doesn't exist. Your best move is to get a hold of your cash flow and save the 20 percent, working with your numbers as they actually exist.

Though the One-Number Budget is simple, the world around you is not. You also need to be prepared to combat the financial foes that threaten to derail your commitment to living within your One Number.

Chapter 7

BEWARE OF
FINANCIAL VAMPIRES

Do you know about energy vampires?

Even if you've never heard the term, I'm sure that you know who they are. These are the people who just suck the life out of you after each interaction. When you see this person's number come up on your cell phone, you breathe in sharply and feel your shoulders rise, because you know that they're going to spend the next hour spouting off a long list of all the horrible things that have been happening to them.

They're extraordinary complainers—everything from car trouble to coworkers is on the table—but it's more than that. Every interaction with an energy vampire leaves you feeling tapped out, completely sucked dry of all your emotional energy. It's why we call them vampires: they really do just suck the life out of you.

You might be saying to yourself, "Okay, John, why don't you just ignore them? Don't pick up the phone, and cut all those energy vampires out of your life for good?"

Fair question. The thing is, an energy vampire isn't a monster or an enemy that you hate. It's actually a person that you love. It could be your college roommate, or your best friend at the office, or even your dear old mom or dad. We *love* these people, or else we wouldn't let them do this to us.

There are financial vampires out there, too. These are things that you spend money on because you have an emotional connection to them. You may want them because they provide a hit of pleasure, status, or security. You may also want them because someone—or more likely, some corporate entity—is manipulating your emotions around certain purchases. Whether they come in the form of impulse purchases, big-ticket must-haves, or consumer debt, these financial vampires can bleed you dry and work against your ability to accumulate wealth.

FINANCIAL VAMPIRES TO AVOID

Your personal energy vampires might be different from mine. You might like solving problems for friends but be totally drained by hearing about their intense stamp collecting hobby. Financial vampires are similar: everyone has a different weakness. The key is to identify yours and start paying close attention to how you react when they come up. Vampires lurk in darkness but can't survive long once you shine a light on them, so be honest with yourself about which ones have been feeding off your budget.

Madison Avenue Purchases

Madison Avenue purchases is my name for consumer spending that is driven by emotion. This is when you just *want* something. Very often that want has been created for you by the advertising industry, which—as any *Mad Men* fan knows—was historically based on Madison Avenue in New York.

These people are very good at their jobs, and advertising is *everywhere*. It's not just a couple TV spots anymore, because advertising is also embedded into social media, YouTube, podcasts, product placement on TV and in movies, and sponsored content where you think someone is just showing off their fun new gizmo, but they've actually been paid to talk (and post) about it.

Advertisers are a sophisticated bunch, and they are *constantly* finding new ways to get you to part with your money and give it to whatever they're promoting. They understand human psychology better than anybody and know how to position their products to get you to buy them.

You're being manipulated.

Retailers are excellent at positioning their products for impulse purchases. One of my favorite examples of this is the mini deep fryer. Every time I go to Target, I'm on the lookout for shopping carts with this little appliance in them—and I'm almost never disappointed. That's because this particular appliance is usually positioned on an end cap along the main aisle, where everyone is sure to see it. It's got a price point that you don't have to worry too much about—usually $19.95, which is spelled out in big, bold lettering. The box always features a photo of a beautifully prepared basket of French fries that just look delicious.

All of this put together pushes a lot of buttons in unsuspecting shoppers' brains. There's serendipity: the product just shows up in front of you, like the purchase was meant to be! There's the low price, which lowers your guard and makes you feel wealthy for being able to treat yourself. There's also the promise of a delicious meal, which triggers your very deep-seated need for nourishment.

I almost always see someone walk out of the store with a countertop appliance that will almost certainly end up on the bargain table at their next tag sale. You will never convince me that these people woke up that morning and thought, "Today is the day I get the deep fryer." No way. It's an impulse purchase, and that impulse was carefully created and managed by the dark powers of advertising.

The same thing happens online, by the way, when ads keep popping up for a product you researched, when you get email reminders from retailers, and when your social media feed is filled with products exactly suited to your taste. Advertising is everywhere, and you may be more susceptible to it than you think.

Car Dealerships

Speaking of buying things you don't need: car companies are always trying to convince you to get into a new car, even though the one you have still gets you from point A to point B. They spend a lot on advertising, but what they're really selling you is the monthly payment rather than a clear look at what that new car will cost when all is said and done.

Your friendly neighborhood car salesman would be broke if he had to sell you a $40,000 item. That's pretty easy to say no to, because it's a huge number. So instead, he changes the game to focus on how much it will cost you per month. If that's just a $150 change in cash flow, you feel like you can afford it easily—just like that $19.95 mini deep fryer. Once you decide you like the car, the salesman will probe to find out your current monthly payment and get a sense of how much *more* you could afford to spend on top of that. If your current car payment is $350 per month, he'll try to push you to $500. You'll find a way to part with an extra $150 per month, and you walk out of there feeling like you got a good deal.

What this interaction isn't telling you is the full impact of that additional $150 per month. Over the course of a five-year car loan, you've spent $9,000 more than you would have if you stuck with your $350 monthly payment. Even worse, if you were almost done paying off your original car, you could have had $350 per month back in your pocket. Over five years, that's another $21,000 that you could have invested or put toward something else that you care about: a down payment on a house, saving for college, or turbocharging your wealth building.

The commonly accepted cycle of financing and replacing a car every five years is one that will ultimately leave you tens—and even *hundreds* —of thousands of dollars poorer. If you can hang on to that car for even seven years instead of five, you end up with many payment-free years that leave you with more money to invest. Let's take a look at how this plays out over one 35-year period.

Let's assume that, during your Middle 30 earning years, you buy a new car every five years. Each time you do it, you finance $30,000. The interest rate on that loan is 2.99 percent, but that's not the only money you lose in this transaction. There's also something that economists call a **lost opportunity cost**. This is the return that you *could have made* on this money if you had invested it elsewhere instead of using it to pay for your car. For the sake of argument, let's say that your lost opportunity cost is 6.5 percent.

When we start to tally up the interest rate of the financing as well as the lost opportunity cost over the years, you begin to see just how expensive buying a new car every five years really is:

Cost of Buying a New Car Every 5 Years

Amount Financed: **$30,000**   Months of Loan: **60**
Finance Rate: **2.99%**   Monthly Payment: **($537.59)**
LOC Rate: **6.50%**   Annual (Monthly x 12): **$6,451**

Buy a new car every 5 years and finance for 5 years

AGE	YEARS	COST
34	5	$36,730
39	10	$87,053
44	15	$156,001
49	20	$250,464
54	25	$379,888
59	30	$557,209
64	35	$800,155

Figure 10: New car financing expense report

Now, what would happen if you only bought and financed a new car every seven years? Over the course of 35 years, you'll only buy five cars instead of seven, but your cumulative savings are much greater than just the sticker price of those two vehicles:

Cost Comparison of Buying a New Car Every 5 Years vs. Every 7 Years

Amount Financed: **$30,000**
Finance Rate: **2.99%**
LOC Rate: **6.50%**

Months of Loan: **60**
Monthly Payment: **($537.59)**
Annual (Monthly x 12): **$6,451**

Difference at Age 64: **$180,547**

Buy a new car every 5 years and finance for 5 years			Buy a new car every 7 years and finance for 5 years (2 years no payment)			CUMULATIVE SAVINGS
AGE	YEARS	COST	AGE	YEARS	COST	
34	5	$36,730	34	5	$36,730	$0
39	10	$87,053	39	10	$70,962	$16,092
44	15	$156,001	44	15	$119,766	$36,234
49	20	$250,464	49	20	$194,369	$56,095
54	25	$379,888	54	25	$294,733	$85,154
59	30	$557,209	59	30	$425,431	$131,778
64	35	$800,155	64	35	$619,607	$180,547

Figure 11: New car financing expense report

In this scenario, we can see that buying a car every seven years is far less expensive than buying one every five years. (For a full accounting of exactly how this works, see the expanded spreadsheet in the Appendix.) When you crunch the numbers to include interest payments and opportunity cost, you end up saving $180,547 over the course of your earning years.

That's the *true* cost of buying and financing a new car every five years. Over the course of your lifetime, it has a major negative impact on your finances—and it is hidden in plain sight!

Financial Institutions

It may seem counterintuitive that financial institutions are a financial vampire. Shouldn't they be the ones helping you to meet your goals? They can definitely be helpful, but they are also trying to make money— and that profit comes from you, primarily by servicing your debt.

In the moment, debt always seems like it's presenting you with the opportunity of choice. You have the option to buy that new car, mini deep fryer, or anything else your heart desires *right now*. As you continue to accumulate debt, however, it actually reduces your choices and you become a prisoner to it. Eventually you have to pay the piper, and future payments will eventually prevent you from making choices about how you want to live. This is especially true the day those paychecks finally stop.

Debt also keeps you from putting your money toward wealth building *today*. If you put $1,000 toward credit card debt each month, you can't use that money to boost your savings rate. And if you've already hit your 20 percent savings goal, that $1,000 could be put toward giving yourself a better life that month—but you can't because you have to send it to the credit card company. Your choices are limited because your funds are spoken for.

If you're feeling the pinch of credit card debt right now, it's worth pointing out that your younger self did this. You're feeling the pain of being robbed, so you know it sucks. Keep this in mind when you are tempted to dip into the pockets of your future self to buy something today.

But you didn't act alone: credit cards aided and abetted the theft of your wealth. If you're dealing with credit card debt, you're not alone: in 2020, the average American had a consumer debt balance of $92,727.[8] It's also important to remember that debt doesn't just come in the form of credit cards. It can also wheedle its way into your life in the form of a home equity line of credit, auto loans, and student loans—including those nearly unlimited PLUS loans that parents take out to send the kids to their dream college. (We'll talk more about college in the next chapter.)

Other financial vampires include the fees banks charge for the use of their products, whether it's a minimum balance fee, ATM fee, or late payment fee. These can add up if you're not careful, and it's especially galling when they happen on an account or credit card you're not even using anymore.

Although it's absolutely critical to protect your Human Life Value with the right insurance coverages, insurance companies can sometimes act as financial vampires. This is often the case with policies that bank

---

[8] Stolba, Stefan Lembo. "Average U.S. Consumer Debt Reaches New Record in 2020." Experian. 6 April 2021. https://www.experian.com/blogs/ask-experian/research/consumer-debt-study/.

on very rare events, such as cancer insurance or supplemental policies with a very limited scope for payouts. These specialty products are often an emotional purchase, but when you do the math on what you pay in premiums versus the amount of help you'll actually receive if you need it, you're losing money on the deal.

Finally, financial speculation is another vampire that can have disastrous results. It can be tempting to read a few articles and plow some of your extra money into certain stocks, cryptocurrency, or a real estate investment on your own, but short-term gains are typically lost over time. Your day trading portfolio could be up by 30 percent right now, but eventually things even out, and you'll end up back where you started. Betting on the stock market or Bitcoin is gambling, not investing, and more often than not it's a drain on your finances.

Real Estate

It's easy to think that a mortgage is different from other types of loans, or that a real estate investment is somehow less risky than the stock market or other types of financial speculation. It's not. You're still borrowing money, and you need to be very careful to put the monthly payment into perspective over the course of your entire life.

One common mistake people make with real estate is to switch houses frequently. Buying and selling houses is a costly proposition, because the real estate agent likes to get paid. On a $500,000 house, the 6 percent brokerage fee is $30,000, and doing that every five years is going to add up quick. If your house doesn't skyrocket in value the way you hope, you could end up underwater or barely break even when you go to sell. If you're thinking of moving within the next five years, you should consider renting.

THE LESSON

Financial vampires are sneaky because they tend to shave just a little off your budget here and there, but those expenses add up to enormous sums of money over the course of a lifetime. Financial vampires come in the form of consumer spending and several forms of debt, and they always make you feel like they're not that expensive.

The key to driving a stake through the heart of these vampires is to stick to your own agenda. You know your One Number, and you don't have to be swayed by the notion that you can afford to extract just a little more from your cash flow. Your One Number keeps your lifetime cash flow at the forefront of your planning and is a powerful weapon against anyone who tries to convince you that you can afford something based on a low monthly payment. It's how much it costs your future self that really matters.

Many people get off track financially because they allow others—advertisers, salespeople, and financial institutions—to set their agenda for them. When you use the One-Number Budget, you've set your own agenda. You know what you have to do, so it's like drawing a line in the sand. I like to picture that statue of the little girl staring down the bull on Wall Street. She has her hands on her hips, chin thrust out, and she's standing her ground. That's you versus your financial vampires.

You can do it. My hope is that the One-Number Budget empowers you to plant your flag and say no to financial vampires. In doing that, you're saying yes to your financial future.

Saying no to faceless ad men and bank CEOs is one thing, but some decisions are even harder—especially when they involve the people you love.

Chapter 8

BEWARE OF
SPENDING FOR
LOVE

As a financial advisor, I sometimes mentor younger colleagues to help them get started in their careers. In this hypothetical example, a brand-new advisor asked me to sit in on an initial consultation with a potential client. All I knew walking into the meeting was that the client had about $250,000 to invest, and my young colleague really wanted to impress this gentleman and hopefully turn him into a client. He asked me along to help walk the client through the process of financial planning.

After the standard meet-and-greet conversation, we sat down to take a look at the client's finances. The man was about 55 years old and a very successful lawyer with a gross income of $400,000 per year. At first glance, he appeared to be doing very well.

But then we began to dig a little deeper into his finances. As I ran the numbers, it was clear that his current net worth was *way* lower than what I would expect from someone who makes as much as he did.

I started asking him some questions. One of the things he shared with me—and I will never forget the pride in his voice as he said it—was that he had promised his children that they could go anywhere they wanted for their education. Not just the college of their dreams, but also any private high school they liked.

He had six children.

Immediately I could see why he only had $250,000 to his name: all of his money was going toward tuition.

I got to work creating a cash flow plan to show him the effects of his promise on his ability to save for retirement. His $250,000 in savings would, at best, get him through a year or two of retirement before he was completely broke—especially if he remained committed to his current level of spending on tuition. I explained to him exactly what I laid out for you in Chapter 4, showing how he would outlive his money mountain if he didn't make some changes.

This was a gentleman who clearly loved his children, and I had to tell him that his best-case scenario was that he died at his desk at the age of 80. He would never be able to retire at this rate, regardless of how his money was invested. He would have to work at the same intense pace until he was an old man—assuming his health allowed him to do so, which of course is never guaranteed.

Much to the horror of the young advisor who had asked for my help, I brought the discussion to a close. Instead of steering the conversation toward investment strategies, I told him this:

"I understand you made a promise to your kids, but I have a really hard time believing that your family would want you to keep that promise if they knew what it would cost you. If they were sitting here with you, looking at how hard you would have to work for the next 25 years, with no end in sight, I can't believe they would be on board with this. Have a family meeting, be honest about these numbers, and see where that conversation goes."

The gentleman smiled, looked down at the table, then looked back at me and smiled again. "I understand everything that you're telling me," he said. "Thank you. But I made a promise and I'm going to keep it."

With that, the meeting ended and I never saw him again.

Whenever I think of him, it always makes me sad. He may not have spent all of his money on fancy vacations and cars, but he robbed his future self all the same. It's even more devastating because he knew he was doing it, and he chose to do it anyway.

For *love.*

It's relatively easy to put your hands on your hips and take a stand against car companies and Madison Avenue guys, but it's very hard to say no to a loved one. Unfortunately, our parents and children can lead us to make some terrible financial decisions, all in the name of love. Some of the biggest pitfalls to growing your wealth are the people you love the most, but you can't let their desires take precedence over your financial security.

SPENDING ON PARENTS

There may come a point in your life when your parents aren't really the adults in your relationship anymore. Whether it's because they are physically or mentally unable to take care of themselves, it's very likely that someday you will have to be the adult and make decisions about their care and finances. This is a very difficult moment, and it gets even harder when money enters the picture. If your parents made mistakes with their finances or have fallen short of their retirement goals, it can quickly derail your own plan if you're not careful.

I've worked with clients whose parents didn't adequately allocate for their own retirement. It's a familiar scene: adults in their forties are working hard, paying for their own mortgage and childcare bills, and taking care of all the other things that come with building a career and raising a family. Then one day, a parent shows up and says, "Hey, I'm having trouble paying some of my bills. Could you help me out?"

For most people, it's very hard to say no. These are your parents after all: they raised you and you love them—or, at least, you have a complex, lifelong relationship with them. You may want to help them, you may feel guilty, you may be angry, or you may be overwhelmed. You may feel all of these things. Because close relationships and intense emotions are involved, it's very hard to think clearly.

But please remember this: any solution you find needs to work within your One Number, or else someday you'll be asking your kids to bail you out, too.

There are many reasons why a parent may come to you for help. Maybe they have an unanticipated health problem they're dealing with, or they didn't expect to become a caregiver to a sick spouse. Maybe they tapped out their own savings acting as the caregiver for their own parents. Or maybe they've never been great with money and have spent far more than they've saved. The details may or may not matter to you. Your parents gave you life, you love them, and you want to help them.

The unfortunate truth is that your household economics do not change because people you love are experiencing a financial challenge. The vast majority of American households have a finite amount of lifetime earnings. When another household reaches into your lifetime earnings, it creates a headwind that—depending on how big the need is—you might not be able to power through.

Setting limits to keep yourself financially strong is important not just for your immediate family but also for the folks that are asking you for help. If you maintain your financial strength, then you will also be able to maintain the role of helper. If you don't, you won't be in a position to help anyone—and will end up looking for help yourself.

If your parent truly cannot live without your help, I recommend sponsoring a bill and paying it directly. The biggest impact you can have is to take over their rent by paying it directly to the landlord. This provides them with a place to live and frees up their money that was previously going towards rent for other living expenses. Often, if you take housing costs out of their budget, they can make a life for themselves out of Social Security income and whatever other money they may have access to. This strategy also protects you by putting a limit on your cash outflow. You will be able to plan your spending and avoid having to come to the rescue for additional unforeseen bills. By directly taking over their housing needs, you've provided for your loved one while putting a cap on your monthly outlay at the same time.

If you can't afford the full rent, maybe you can offer to pay half. Or perhaps you can cover utilities. Every situation is different, and you'll have to take a hard look at your One Number to find a solution that works for you. You can help your parents within limits—just make sure you know exactly what those limits are, and stick to them.

This type of situation often takes people by surprise, because most families don't talk about money, especially between generations. Many adult children get surprised when their parents come to them and share that they are unable to cover their expenses. As difficult as it is for the adult child to hear it, know that it surely wounds the parents' pride to admit it. There's no way to minimize it: this is difficult and painful.

But it's also an opportunity for empowerment. As you take over the role of adult in your relationship with your parents, you can make sure you don't make the same mistakes they did. You can do better, both for yourself and for your children, by sticking to your One Number and making sure your savings rate is high enough to protect your future self.

SPENDING ON COLLEGE

When it comes to spending for love, on one hand you have your parents, and on the other you have your children. I'm a father, and I love my daughter. Of course I want the very best for her—that's what we all want for our children. That's a major reason why spending on college can be the biggest financial mistake parents make in their lives. It certainly was for the lawyer we met at the beginning of this chapter.

I went to college back in the early 1990s. I attended Susquehanna University, a beautiful little school in the middle of Pennsylvania. When my parents dropped me off, we spent the morning unloading my stuff into my freshman dorm room. When the last bags were in the building, I went back out to the car with my parents to say goodbye. My mom got out her camera and looked over at my dad.

My father was not a hugger. He was born in 1929, and he was, to be honest, an emotionally awkward guy. I was dreading posing for the official Right of Passage photo and saying goodbye to my parents, because I just *knew* the next five minutes were going to be uncomfortable for us.

My mom snapped the photo, and my dad just stuck out his hand. I shook it.

"You've got four years," he said. "The clock's ticking."

With that, he got into the car and drove off.

My dad is never going to win any awards for being warm and fuzzy, but he actually gave me a huge gift that day. I knew in no uncertain terms that I had to graduate on time. There was no bottomless well of tuition money for me.

Fast forward to today, and colleges are bragging about their *six*-year graduation rates, while tuition has skyrocketed. There are now entire departments designed around undeclared majors, and no one seems to think this is a problem.

Full disclosure: *I* think this is a problem. I believe that college as a concept has been oversold to the American people. Colleges want your money, and so do the banks who do all the lending that has led to massive student debt. Education is important, of course. But with private college sticker prices pushing $65,000 and higher per year, it is up to you to determine what is reasonable for you and your family *within the context of your One Number.*

I'm not about to tell anyone where or whether to go to college. Like all of your lifestyle spending choices, college comes out of your One Number, and it is up to you to set your financial priorities within that number. But I will point out that in today's dollars, my four years at that small private college in Pennsylvania costs $200,000, whereas my graduate degree at a state school (George Mason University—go Patriots!) costs less than half that amount. Having experienced both a public and private university, I'm here to tell you that I don't believe I would be any less successful today if I had gone to a state school at the age of 18.

Let me repeat: college spending comes out of your One Number. *It is not part of your 20 percent savings rate.* That's for wealth building, and it's meant to protect your future self. Spending on your loved ones comes out of your One Number, so this decision must work for both your present and your future self.

To do that, both you and your child have to look at the long-term impacts of your family's college decision. You already know how to work with your One Number, so do the math and see what you can afford to part with when it comes to your lifestyle expenses.

Next, it's time to teach your children about the One-Number Budget. No kid has any real idea of what $100,000 in debt actually means. Remember, most *adults* have trouble understanding what numbers that big mean in the context of lifetime cash flow, so few teenagers are likely to grasp this concept without help.

So show them.

Estimate a reasonable, entry-level salary in their major and use that for the income number, then work the One-Number Budget from there. For undeclared majors, assume $40,000 per year.

When you get to the fixed expenses, take out 15 percent for housing first. Then add the monthly student loan payment that your child can count on based on the financial aid package at their dream school. (You can use a loan calculator to get the details right.) The remaining amount is what they have left to eat, drive, and keep the lights on.

A quick, back-of-the-envelope example: $100,000 of student debt at 5 percent interest financed over a 20-year period results in a $657 monthly loan payment. Will someone making only $40,000 a year be able to handle that type of payment? Does starting life $657 in the hole—every month from graduation day until they turn 42—really make any sense?

Let's use the One-Number Budget to find out:

Jordan's One-Number Budget

Gross Household Income (annual):	$40,000	
Wealth Building for Retirement = 20%	X .20	= $8,000
Taxes (Federal, State, Local, Real Estate) = 20%	X .20	= $8,000
Lifestyle Expenses = 60%	X .60	= $24,000
Total Monthly Lifestyle Expenses	÷ 12 = $2,000	
Less Housing: (15% of $40,000 ÷ 12)	– $500	
Less Other Fixed Expenses (student loans, etc.)	– $657	
Jordan's One-Number Budget for the Month:	**Total: $843**	

Note: The above calculations and percentages are for illustrative purposes only and are not deemed to be used as tax advice. For tax advice specific to your situation, please contact a CPA or tax attorney for help.

Figure 12: One-Number Budget example

When Jordan, our recent college grad, breaks down their income according to the One-Number Budget, it's clear that being on the hook for $657 in student loan payments every month doesn't leave that much to live on. And lest you think that income-based repayment options are the solution, you should know that Jordan will pay way more over the life of the loan, and insufficient career income could mean that Jordan *never* pays off the loan.

It's also worth noting that I've tweaked the One-Number Budget above to account for a young person's lower tax burden, and Jordan *still* only has $843 left each month to pay for Wi-Fi, food, and gas for the car, along with anything else they'll need.

It may well be that Jordan can get by on that amount by living with roommates and driving a less expensive used car, but what happens when friends come up with plans for fun? Concerts, vacations, and birthday dinners at a nice restaurant all cost extra. These things are hard to say no to—especially when you're young—so they inevitably end up coming out of the 20 percent Jordan is supposed to be saving. Pretty soon Jordan is just like the man in the poem who robbed his future self to enjoy today.

This is an important wake-up call.

Think of the One-Number Budget as a tool for introducing your child to their future self. Walking through the numbers is the best way I know to make the impact of student loans as real as possible. Remember, lenders don't want you to think about the lifetime impact of these loans. They're banking on making an emotional sale. The One-Number Budget keeps your future self—and your child's future—in the conversation.

SPENDING ON ADULT CHILDREN

One of the reasons you may be tempted to overspend on college is to ensure your child's success. But no matter what you do, you could find yourself welcoming—or at least, begrudgingly accepting—a boomerang child back into your life.

Boomerang children are adults who, after college or at some point in their lives, move back in with their parents. This happens for all sorts of reasons: high rent, unemployment, a medical crisis, a bad breakup—you never know. You tried to launch your adult child out into the world, but for one reason or another, they landed right back at your doorstep.

As a hypothetical example, I once worked with a married couple that was having a hard time and were hoping to find a way to get back on track financially. In our first meeting, I could tell right away that their marriage was about to end. They were under enormous strain because the husband was unemployed, and his prospects didn't look good. Even though the wife had a good, steady paycheck, they had serious cash flow problems. It was clear that his self-esteem had taken a hit, and that she was sick of the whole situation and of trying to make ends meet.

I should mention that I think one of the saddest things in the world is watching a marriage fall apart. One of the biggest stressors on a marriage is money, and I take seriously the fact that my work can ease that burden and, hopefully, keep families intact. So I very much wanted to help this pair find a solution to their problem.

As we talked over the basics of their cash flow, I heard many references to Timmy. "Who's Timmy?" I finally asked.

"He's our son."

I was a little confused, because there had been no talk of childcare expenses or saving for college. "How old is Timmy?" I asked.

"Twenty-six."

Huh?

"He's a good kid," the man explained. "He's just the kind of guy who needs time to find himself, you know?"

The good news is that Timmy had a job of sorts. He taught guitar lessons as a casual, cash-under-the-table-type of gig.

"So how much does Timmy pull down a year?" I asked.

"$50,000."

I did my best not to let my jaw hit the floor, but I'm not sure I succeeded. Here was this couple under enormous strain and unable to make ends meet, and their adult son was living rent-free and making $50,000 in untaxed income. He didn't help with a single bill. He didn't even do his own laundry!

This couple was waiting for the moment when Timmy finally felt ready to move out and live on his own. But here's the thing: Timmy was *never* going to leave because he could never duplicate what his parents were providing for free—room, board, valet laundry service, the works. He had no incentive to do anything to change the status quo.

To his credit, Timmy did start paying rent once I made it clear to his parents that they absolutely needed that income to get back on track with their finances. But the moral of the story is clear: if you're not careful, your adult children can become a huge drain on your finances.

By now, you've probably figured out that any financial support you do provide for them has to come out of your One Number. Just as you would with your aging parents, you need to have clear expectations about what you can afford to do, and you need to draw a firm line in your budget. The rule about taking on a bill instead of handing over cash still stands.

For newly minted college graduates, it might make sense for you to provide rent-free housing for a limited time period. My parents generously did this for me, and I made the most of it by getting myself into a position where I could afford to move out. I got a good job and bought a new car, but I applied the amount I would have been paying for an apartment to that loan—probably $650 or $700 a month at the time—to aggressively pay off the loan. Once the car was paid off, that freed up $700 each month in cash flow to pay my rent, and I was able to move out just 20 months after I graduated.

If it makes sense for you, offering your child a rent-free period can help them knock out a big portion of their student loans. You'd have to make a clear deal about how much of their income they put toward the loans in exchange for living in their childhood bedroom, but allowing them to kill their debt is one way to set them up for financial success.

Again, I strongly recommend pairing this with a good financial education. You want to show them the One-Number Budget and get them in the habit of saving and understanding lifetime cash flow from day one. You also want to have a clearly defined exit strategy whenever an adult child moves back in with you.

We all want to help our kids, but helping them doesn't have to mean doing everything for them. Keep an eye on your One Number and be clear about what you can do, and you'll put yourself in a position of strength when it comes to helping your loved ones with life's challenges. You'll also be giving your children an incredible gift, and one that their future selves will thank you for: you will have enough cash to care for yourself and never become a burden on them. This will make it that much easier for your kids to become and remain financially independent, breaking intergenerational cycles of shame and resentment. You'll be able to just enjoy each other, instead of worrying about how to keep everyone afloat.

THE LESSON

Spending for love is one of the hardest things to say no to. The most common blind spots in financial decision-making involve taking care of aging parents, making decisions about children's education, and supporting adult children.

It's only natural to want the best for the people you love, but it's critical to your financial well-being that you say no when you need to. This requires you to have a clear vision of what you are able to spend, and the strength to stick to your plan. Remember, your 20 percent savings are for your future self. Any additional spending on your children or parents *must* come out of your One Number.

You know that line you hear on an airplane about putting on your own oxygen mask before you help the person in the seat next to you? Your One Number is your financial oxygen mask. It's not selfish to take care of your own needs first—doing so is precisely what will allow you to best take care of the people you love. If you jeopardize your future wealth by overspending on parents or children now, soon you won't be able to take care of *anyone*. Your One Number lets you know what you can afford. The trick is to stick to it.

I often think about that lawyer who just couldn't bring himself to place any type of limits on his children's educational choices. Maybe more than anyone I've met, he is the victim of the thief from the poem. This man's love for his children blinded him to the reality of the future. His younger self picked his future pockets clean to pay for private school and college, and he will never be able to retire as a result. He probably won't even be able to keep his promise to all of his children, because eventually life will get in the way and he will have to stop working. We all do, eventually, either by choice or by circumstance.

But what if he had been able to see that his lifetime cash flow would never be enough to pay for six private college tuitions? What if he had been able to accept that his money mountain was never going to catch up to the forces seeking to erode it? He might have said, "Let's not do private high school." He might have paid for half of his children's college expenses, and let them work for or borrow the rest. With more skin in the game, those kids might have made very different choices, too.

I can't believe that this man's family actually wanted him to die at his desk. What they really wanted was his time—just like your family does. Having an honest discussion would have made those options clear, but he skipped over that discussion and instead doomed himself to insurmountable debt.

You don't have to make this same mistake.

By taking a long-term view of your cash flow, you can see what money might be available over your lifetime and make decisions accordingly. And once you get real about money with your family and decide what you can afford to spend on them, you're ready to face down one last person who's trying to steal from your future self.

To see that person, all you need to do is look in the mirror.

Chapter 9

BEWARE OF PSYCHOLOGICAL PITFALLS

It took me 10 years to lose 20 pounds.

After a serious conversation with my doctor about my cholesterol, I knew I needed to make a big change. There's really no secret to losing weight, and we all know what we need to do: move more and eat less. But after I lost the first 10 pounds, I got stuck. I just couldn't get past that plateau.

Finally, I went to see a nutritionist. I wasn't getting anywhere on my own anymore, so I knew I needed help. Among other things, she taught me that a calorie of protein is a lot different than a calorie of croissant. She provided specialized knowledge and set me up with a nutrition plan and some homework: a food diary.

When we next met, she was very no-nonsense about my food diary. "What are these peanut M&Ms all about, John? Those aren't anywhere on the list of foods I gave you."

So I explained all about the bad day I'd had, and how a call with a client hadn't gone well. It made me sad, so I hit the vending machine to make myself feel better. This, by the way, is where food lives in my life. I use it for celebrations with family and friends, and I also use it for comfort when things don't go well.

"No more of that!" she said. "The next time that happens, you're gonna go outside and take a walk. You are *not* going to hit the vending machine. Do something else until the urge passes."

I listened to her advice, and it worked. She knew I had developed a pattern of behavior that connected food and feelings, and she wanted me to interrupt those patterns to build new ones. In addition to her specialized knowledge, my nutritionist provided coaching specific to my personal situation. It was delivered at the exact moment I needed it, so I finally got results.

I share this story because I know firsthand just how hard it is to change habits, even when you know the change is in your best interests. It's so easy to make an excuse so you feel better in the moment, but following this advice was life-changing. When I did it, I felt more powerful and in control—a feeling that grew as the number of good food decisions I made mounted and the weight came off. My confidence grew, and soon I was riding momentum and experiencing real success after so many false starts.

If you're having trouble getting started, try again. I know you can do it. Whether you're working to manage cash flow or calories, the truth is that there's no secret or silver bullet. You know what you need to do—but you may have patterns of thoughts and behaviors that are holding you back. The final barrier to saving for retirement is often in your own mind, so it's important to understand the psychology and emotions tied up in your money.

DELAYED GRATIFICATION

Human beings aren't really wired for delayed gratification, so just telling someone to do the right thing now so it pays off later isn't very helpful. In the diet and exercise world, this is closely tied to evolution. When we lived in caves and had no refrigerators, we never knew when our next meal was coming. So when the food was there, we ate as much as we could. That's a great strategy for cavemen, but not so much for modern people who have full pantries and food delivery apps. There's no scarcity, so when we pack on the pounds, they stay firmly in place around our midsections instead of getting burned off for energy in times of famine.

Because our brains are still wired like cavemen, we also act out this scenario with our finances. For example, consider the worker who gets a big bonus check one year. Since she doesn't know when or if she'll ever get another windfall like that, the temptation is to spend it now. Might as well enjoy it, because you never know when you'll get another chance, right?

In the case of the bonus check, delayed gratification would protect your future self from financial famine, but it's hard to overcome the feeling that you need to spend that money now to make the most of it. This is why the One-Number Budget is so powerful: you treat every windfall the same way you do your regular income. Take 20 percent off the top for your savings, set aside 30 percent for taxes (if this hasn't already been withheld for you), and the rest is yours to enjoy. The delayed gratification is already built in with your 20 percent savings rate, so you don't have to feel financially starved. You're allowed to enjoy some abundance—as long as you stay with your One Number.

THE PLEASURE PRINCIPLE

One of the reasons delayed gratification is challenging is because we all want to be happy. One of the biggest drivers of human behavior is the pleasure principle:[9] our desire to seek pleasure and avoid pain.

The pleasure principle is what makes spending so irresistibly *fun*. It's fun to go on vacations, drive nice cars, and go out to eat in a fancy restaurant. And any financial advice that ignores this basic psychological truth is destined to fail.

For example, I like to go out to eat with my wife. Let's say that a really fancy night out with candlelight, a bottle of wine, and a couple of steaks costs us $200. A lot of financial gurus out there will tell you that this is a total waste of money, and that you could have the exact same meal, while only spending $45 at the grocery store.

They are missing the point.

It's not about the steak. It's about the atmosphere, doing something special with my wife, and not having to clean the kitchen afterward. It's something we do together to enjoy one another's company. The pleasure of that evening goes beyond just the cost of the meat on the

---

[9] "APA Dictionary of Psychology." American Psychological Association. https://dictionary.apa.org/pleasure-principle.

plate, and advising people to forego those pleasures is never going to work.

It's also important to recognize that a lot of our pleasure in spending revolves around creating community. Family vacations allow us to reconnect with loved ones. Hanging out at the mall is a way to spend time with friends. A technophile's gadget purchase might help her feel like part of a community of gamers or cellphone fans. It's not for me to decide what gives you pleasure—but I *do* know that you need it in your life. So use the One-Number Budget to make sure you get to spend time with the people you love, doing what you love to do. Just don't spend beyond your means to do it.

EMOTIONAL SPENDING

The pleasure principle is a pretty simple way to understand a lot of human behavior, but it doesn't explain everything. There are often other emotions tied up in how we relate to money, and these can be harder to unpack.

Love

I already talked a lot about spending for love in Chapter 8 and how these emotionally driven decisions can leave you broke if you don't put up some guardrails.

But college isn't the only thing people overspend on. As parents, we just want to make our kids happy and give them opportunities that we may not have had in our own childhood. The desire to provide for our children is huge, and it's what keeps us motivated to make sure they get what they need.

Once you move past the basic needs of food, clothing, and shelter, the wants are endless. Whether it's footing the bill for private tutors, sleepaway camp, semi-professional travel teams, or giving Junior the keys to a new car when he gets his license, it all costs a *lot*. It's hard to say no to your child, because it can feel like you're saying you don't love them.

But here's the thing: you have to be willing to say no to some of their wants in order to remain financially strong enough to meet all of their needs. If you go beyond your financial capacity with your children, you will be a hero today, but in the end you risk becoming financially dependent on the very people you wish to help. As we've discussed in Chapter 8, if you end up needing help during your retirement, you'll be burdening your adult children at the very time when they can least afford to help you, because they'll be putting their own children through college by then. Becoming and staying financially strong yourself isn't selfish—it's actually one of the most loving things you can do for your children.

Entitlement

One of the reasons saying no is difficult is because spending on your children is often tangled up in keeping up with the Joneses. In today's social media–driven culture, there's a lot of pressure to do what everyone else is doing. You're bombarded by photos of the great vacations other families are taking, or the slick new horseback riding school that Mitzi's kids are attending. If everyone else is doing it, you don't want to miss out.

Entitlement isn't a pretty word, but it's something we all feel at some point. You work hard (or you grew up a certain way, or you live in a certain neighborhood), so you *should* have these things! You earned it, people expect it, so why not go get it?

Entitlement is a tricky feeling, because we don't often call it out for what it is. Instead, we rationalize ways to get what we think we should have: "The fancy gym membership is only $150 more each month" or "I deserve a vacation to escape my terrible job for a couple weeks" or—and here's the real doozy—"I'm not sure we can afford it, but we'll figure it out."

Every time I've ever had a client say, "We'll figure it out," it meant that they were actually pushing the numbers to the back of their mind. That money was inevitably stolen from their future selves. Fortunately, knowing your One Number makes it easy to actually do the figuring to see if you can absorb a cost or not. If you are able to tap into a reservoir of cash that was previously not on your radar screen—perhaps a gift, inheritance, or income from a side gig—that's a fine solution. But what you must not do is cut into your 20 percent savings or cash out some of your retirement funds to feed a lifestyle that you can't actually afford.

Fear

Fear is the flip side of the pleasure principle, and it causes us to spend in all kinds of irrational ways. As much as you want to enjoy life, you also desperately want to avoid pain and discomfort—and you'll spend to allay those fears.

Your fears are as unique as you are, and many of them come from your childhood experience. Some of these are easy to recognize: if you lived in a dangerous neighborhood as a child, you may want to spend on a state-of-the-art security system to feel safe in your home as an adult. Most of us also enjoy a healthy dose of escapism to block out the difficult or scary things in our lives. Whether your escape is a fancy vacation or several monthly subscriptions to streaming services, it's worth noting that your spending on these items may be driven by more than just enjoyment.

But some of our fears about money are buried under the surface. They're harder to recognize, but they still influence our behavior.

You've probably internalized your parents' emotions about money. If your parents struggled to make ends meet, you may have a fear of investing (because you don't want to lose your principal), or you may fear living a life of deprivation so you run up the credit card to surround yourself with the things you never had. If your parents never talked about money—and many people of older generations definitely adhered to this taboo—you may have internalized the idea that money is bad, so you shouldn't think about it or even work to save a lot of it.

Everyone's family is different, and your reaction to your childhood could be the exact opposite of your sibling's reaction to the same childhood. It's worth thinking about how your family's beliefs and expectations about money have shaped you so you can recognize your own fears and hang-ups, which is the first step in breaking any bad spending habits you have developed.

PATTERN INTERRUPTIONS

Remember how I was only able to lose those last 10 pounds after I worked with a nutritionist? Her specialized knowledge and personalized coaching helped me to understand my bad eating habits so I could interrupt my pattern of behavior and replace it with something better.

You can do the same thing with your finances.

As I've said before, I never want to tell people how to spend their money. What you do with your One Number is up to you. But what I *can* do is share some best practices that I know will help you pause and think before you spend, so that sticking to your One Number is a little easier.

Weigh Wants versus Needs

Before spending, it's helpful to do a mental check on whether the item is a need or a want. We're so used to saying things like "I need a new TV," but that's not true. Remember that your basic needs are food, shelter, and safety; everything else is a want. It can be helpful to think about your needs according to Maslow's hierarchy:[10]

---

[10] Burton, Neel. "Our Hierarchy of Needs." Psychology Today. 23 May 2012. https://www.psychologytoday.com/us/blog/hide-and-seek/201205/our-hierarchy-needs.

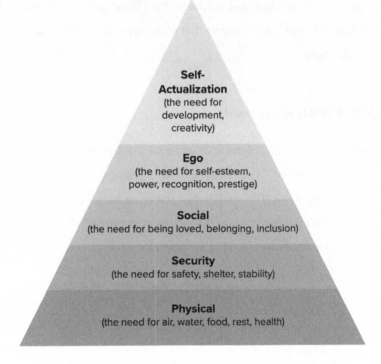

Hierarchy of Needs

Self-Actualization
(the need for development, creativity)

Ego
(the need for self-esteem, power, recognition, prestige)

Social
(the need for being loved, belonging, inclusion)

Security
(the need for safety, shelter, stability)

Physical
(the need for air, water, food, rest, health)

Figure 13: Maslow's hierarchy of needs

As you can see, your basic needs form the foundation of the pyramid, and then things that are more like wants are layered on top. As you consider those wants, it's helpful to ask yourself if they help you meet a psychological or self-actualization need at the top of the pyramid. If it doesn't, it's probably not worth spending on.

When he was young, my aunt encouraged my dad to buy a 1957 Corvette—what I consider to be one of the hottest cars ever built. He did, and I thought that was so awesome when he told me about it years later. But my dad isn't really a car guy, and within two months, the Vette was nothing more than his regular old car. He just didn't care about it. The car didn't fulfill a higher-order need for him, so it didn't change his life.

Tap into Community Support

When I was training for the Marine Corps Urban Ultra, a big 50K race, I told everybody I was doing it. Being public about my goal meant that people would ask me about it, and their interest held me accountable. It would have been way too painful to tell all these people that I gave up and quit, or even that I was slacking off on my training. They were all rooting for me, which provided positive encouragement and a bit of pressure to live up to the expectations I had set.

In the same way, sharing your financial goals with people you trust can provide support and encouragement that keeps you on track. If you tell your friends that you're saving up for a down payment on a house, it can make it easier for you to suggest pizzas and Netflix instead of a night out on the town. They might also just check in with you about how the house hunt is going, which reminds you to stay on track. Meeting goals is easier with a supportive community, and financial goals are no exception.

Create a Safe Environment

I love Oreos, but I can't have them in the house because I will eat the whole box. I'm not proud of this, but that entire box will be gone within 90 minutes. That's why I set myself up with a safe environment at home where I won't be tempted by Oreos. There are lots of ways to make it harder to spend on your biggest temptations. If you love to eat out, limit yourself to one special night per week, and plan the rest of your menus so you have food available to cook. Likewise, if you're in the habit of catching up with friends at the mall, you may want to switch venues so you don't come home with a shopping bag full of impulse purchases.

You want to engineer your environment to make it harder to spend, so consider turning off the auto-renew functions on your subscriptions, and say "no thanks" when online stores ask to save your credit card information. Adding steps to your purchases is a great way to give yourself a second to think before you spend. The more time you give yourself the opportunity to reflect about your spending and ask yourself those wants versus needs questions, the better you'll get at breaking your behavior patterns.

THE LESSON

Losing weight isn't complicated, but it's hard. We all know what we have to do, but—for me, at least—feelings about food can get in the way. I couldn't see how my emotions were driving my behavior until the nutritionist pointed it out and helped me break the patterns.

Your finances are no different. You know what you need to do, and it isn't complicated: save more and spend less. The One-Number Budget strips away the complexity so that you can focus on the hard part: recognizing and overcoming your own psychological traps. By pulling 20 percent off the top of your income and keeping your consumption inside your One Number, you create the financial equivalent of that Oreo-free environment.

You can't overcome your psychological barriers if you're not aware of them, so pay attention. Approach your life with heightened self-awareness so you can figure out where your personal trouble spots are. Whether it's spending for pleasure, love, fear, or entitlement, you have to understand the feelings that drive your spending. Only then can you break old patterns and build new ones by creating a supportive environment and community.

Ready to create solutions that address all the psychological pitfalls that can derail your spending? It all hinges upon having an honest discussion about your goals.

Chapter 10

DISCUSSION WITH YOUR FUTURE SELF

In the financial service industry, we tend to lead with what we sell. That might be life insurance, or a certain type of investment. Whatever it is, that's what we center the discussion around. But in my 20 years of experience as a financial advisor, I have never met anyone who was actually excited about insurance or a mutual fund for its own sake. (And to be honest, if I ever met that person, I'm not sure how well we'd get along with each other!)

What people really want isn't the stocks or the bonds, it's their vision of the future. That's what they're really after—the money is just a way to get there.

So instead of leading with my calculator, I begin every new client meeting with a discussion of their vision for the future. We spend a good half hour on the subject, and I take notes because it's important.

The next day, I memorialize that discussion in a Vision Letter that I send to them, and I always refer back to their vision for context before choosing any particular financial tool or product. The Vision Letter is the touchstone that guides all future financial decisions.

As an example, one day a couple came to me as prospective clients and I took them through the vision discussion. They were in close agreement with each other, and they centered the discussion squarely on the idea of stability. They wanted to make their financial lives more predictable and to feel more secure about their retirement planning. They were both engineers working for government contracting firms, and I knew I could help them reach their goals.

Fast forward a few weeks to another meeting together. When the couple came back to my office, their energy was totally different. "We met this guy who told us that there's a McDonald's franchise opening in a local territory," they said breathlessly. "So we're going to take the $75,000 we have as a cash reserve and use it to buy this McDonald's."

This was totally out of the blue, and they were so excited about it. "Okay," I said, "this is a little bit of a surprise to me." I pulled out their Vision Letter and walked them through the discussion point by point. Nowhere on that paper was any mention of owning a fast-food franchise, or a deep-seated desire to manage teenagers.

If we had never had the vision discussion, this couple could be covering shifts and flipping burgers at a Bethesda McDonald's right now, worrying about the next global pandemic to come their way. It's easy to get excited about a new "opportunity" or the next big thing, whether it's a unique investment opportunity or a career change. Will it hold up? The only way to tell is to look at it in light of your declared vision and who you are as a person.

Fortunately for this couple, we had that letter to anchor our discussions, and it served as a guide to make sure they ended up where they really wanted to be. Your vision keeps you on the right path and prevents you from making financial mistakes.

WRITING YOUR OWN VISION LETTER

Remember all of the financial pitfalls we discussed in Chapters 7 through 9? The best way to avoid them is to have a clear vision of the future you want and an understanding of what financial success means to you. Writing your own Vision Letter is like having a conversation with your future self. It's going to be much harder to steal from someone you've gotten to know, so let's do that work right now.

If we were sitting together in my office, I'd be asking the questions and taking notes while you did all the talking. Since I'm not there in person to do the writing, I want you to take out a pen or pencil and jot your answers down.

Or, if you prefer, you can also download the worksheet at: onenumberbudget.com/worksheet

The important thing is that you think carefully and commit to your answers in writing. That way you can refer to your Vision Letter and use it to check yourself as you continue on your financial journey.

The Big Question

In his work, *Strategic Coach*® founder Dan Sullivan poses what he calls The R-Factor Question®. I have found this to be an incredibly powerful tool in my own life, and it's how I start every vision meeting with clients:

"If we were meeting here 20 years from today, and you were to look back over those 20 years to today, what has to have happened during that period, both personally and professionally, for you to feel happy about your progress?"[11]

This is a *huge* question, and there's a lot to think about. So let's break it down into smaller bites and take it step by step. Sharpen your pencils and take a crack at answering them now.

---

[11] Sullivan, Dan. The Dan Sullivan Question: Ask It and Transform Anyone's Future. Toronto: The Strategic Coach, Inc., 2009.

Six Questions to Focus on Your Future

Imagine you're able to hop in a time machine that takes you 20 years into the future—and everything is *exactly* as you've always wished it to be. You step out of the machine, open your eyes, and look around.

1. Who is there with you? List family members below.

Name	Current Age	Age in 20 Years

Table 1: Blank family members list

2. What activities do you enjoy doing together?

3. Still exploring the world 20 years from now, where are you, and what do you see?

4. What is your professional life like in this time period? Or, if you're retired, how do you spend your time? At what age did you transition out of your full-time career?

5. Before you get back in your time machine, you sneak a peek at your future self's financial statement. What do you see?

6. Back in the time machine, you pause to reflect. What have you just seen in your future that most fills you with joy? What's most important to you?

Getting to the Good Life

Your answers to these questions form your Vision Letter. This is your touchstone that you can refer to any time you make a major decision about your career, your housing, your finances, or anything else that has the potential to change your life—for better or worse. Does the thing you're considering fit in with your vision of the future? Will this decision move you closer to or further away from that vision?

Your Vision Letter will help keep you on track, especially if you're struggling to stay within your One Number. It became clear to the couple who wanted to invest in a McDonald's franchise that owning a fast-food restaurant would definitely *not* add to the feeling of security that underpinned their definition of the good life. Likewise, you can use your Vision Letter to help decide if anything from a Mercedes to a McMansion is truly worth the cost. It might be—but only if it fits into your vision.

Your Vision Letter will also serve as part of your personal GPS. It shows you where you're headed, but it's up to you to map out a route that makes sure you actually arrive. That's where the One-Number Budget comes in. By automatically saving 20 percent of your income before you do anything else, the One-Number Budget keeps you on track to reach your goals. Think of it as insurance for your future self, so that when you finally do meet, you like what you see.

TWO CONVERSATIONS WITH YOUR FUTURE SELF

Now that you have created a clear vision of your future, I want you to do one last imaginative exercise to cement it in your mind. In this exercise you're going to role-play meeting your future self and what that conversation might look like.

Again, take the time to write your answers to solidify your thinking.

Conversation #1: Your Broke Future Self

Imagine a world in which you did *not* save 20 percent of your income. You come face to face with your future self—the one who is living with the consequences of this action (or inaction, as the case may be). Your future self is broke and cannot retire. There is no travel, no hobby, no comfort. Uncertainty about your future is at an all-time high.

1. First, play the role of your broke future self. What is your life like? What does your life look like if you are unable to stop working? Take the time to describe in detail the things you would miss most with a dramatic reduction in your income.

2. Still in the role of your future self, how does this make you feel?

3. Your future self gets one last word. What would you say to your current self about this situation?

4. Now, switch back to being your current self. Look your future self in the face and see their pain. What, if anything, can you say to explain your decision not to save 20 percent of your income?

Conversation #2: Your Successful Future Self

Now, shake off the image of failure and return to your Vision Letter. Reread your answers to those six questions to bring your vision of a successful, happy life back into your mind. This time, imagine that you *did* save 20 percent of your income, and you get to meet the future self who is enjoying the life you worked to build.

1. Play the role of your happy, successful future self. What are the top three things you love about your life?

2. Still in the role of your future self, how does this all make you feel?

3. What would you say to your current self about your life and how you were able to make it happen?

4. Your future self gets the last word this time. What advice
   or words of encouragement do you have for your current
   self?

COMMITTING TO THE
PROJECT

If you completed all the exercises above thoroughly and thought-
fully, congratulations! It takes bravery and consistent work to build
your self-awareness and design a vision for the future, and you now
have a very useful roadmap to guide your thinking about major life
decisions.

If you struggled to develop your vision, I want to acknowledge that
this doesn't come easily to everyone. Lots of people aren't sure
what they want in their lives.

But don't give up. Instead, make developing your Vision Letter an
ongoing project. For the next few weeks, take your best stab at
these questions, maybe working on just one per day. Put it away and
come back to it with a clean piece of paper after a break so you have
time to let your ideas percolate. Then, share your new version with
two or three people who know you well and whose judgment you
respect. Ask them if your vision sounds like you—the real you that
they love, not some person you think you should try to be.

THE LESSON

At the end of the day, the Vision Letter is a continuation of the self-awareness I began talking about in Chapter 9. I want you to get clear on the life that you are designing for yourself so you can then align your financial life to fit with that vision. When you love what you do and your life aligns with your vision, work won't feel like a burden, and you won't be tempted to spend money to escape your life or to heal your psychological wounds.

I was fortunate to see a great example of this type of intentional life when I was young. My tenth-grade English teacher was hands-down the best teacher I ever had, and it was all because he loved being at the school.

But it wasn't always this way.

This man and his wife were once advertising executives on Madison Avenue, but one day they looked at each other and realized that they were deeply unhappy. They did not like their work, and they did not like the people they did that work for.

Instead of grinding it out until they retired, they did the hard thing. They re-engineered their lives. They nearly killed themselves working by day and taking classes at night to become teachers. When they graduated and switched careers, they absolutely loved it. And that's what made them great. They never missed the trappings of success and the big salary, because they were doing what they were made to do. They designed the life they always wanted, and they didn't even have to wait until retirement to feel that way.

So take the time to get grounded in the key pillars of your life that will make you happy—both today and in the future. Then, build your financial life around that vision to give your future self their best shot at happiness.

Once you know what you want, how do you get there? The key is the One-Number Budget and all that you have learned in this book.

CONCLUSION

As a financial advisor, numbers take up a lot of space in my brain. I'm always doing the math, so numbers flow in and flow out, and I'm pretty good at turning off the tap when I go home for the evening. But there are two statistics I just can't stop thinking about.

First, the median household income in the United States is just under $70,000.[12] That means that the average family has this much money to work with each year to cover all of their needs, lifestyle expenses, and saving for the future.

Second, for people aged 55 to 64—the age when so many people decide to come see me for help planning their retirement—the median net worth is $212,500.[13] That amount includes all the money they have in the bank, investments, and any equity they have tied up in their home.

---

[12] Shrider, Emily A. et al. "Income and Poverty in the United States: 2020." United States Census Bureau. 14 September 2021. https://www.census.gov/library/publications/2021/demo/p60-273.html.

[13] DeMatteo, Megan. "Here's the average net worth of Americans ages 65 to 74." CNBC. 5 October 2021. https://www.cnbc.com/select/average-net-worth-of-americans-ages-65-to-74/.

These numbers keep me up at night, because the average family definitely does not have enough saved for retirement. A $212,500 nest egg just isn't going to cut it when they're used to living on $70,000 a year. It might get them through five years without working, and then what? These families will be relying on Social Security, and that's it. At that point, they'll be making less than 50 percent of what they were earning before.

Would a 50 percent reduction in income support *your* vision for the future?

I wrote this book because I want to save families. In my work, I've seen firsthand how the stress of money problems can break up marriages and put strain on the relationships between parents and children. I've met people like the man in the poem at the beginning of the book—people who end up broke and alone in their old age because they robbed themselves of a secure future. There are a million ways to steal from your future self, but only one way to set yourself up for success: cash flow management.

Cash flow management is the most important part of your financial life. There's no two ways about it: you need to master this skill to make sure that your money mountain is evenly spread over your whole life. The money you earn during the Middle 30 has to pay for your living expenses for the last 60 years of your life—the Middle 30 *and* Final 30.

The One-Number Budget is one of the best tools you have to help get this job done. It makes sure that you pay your future self first, and it helps you build the habit of living within the *correct* amount of money each month, so you have plenty to enjoy later. It optimizes your decision-making today so you can work to feel comfortable and secure tomorrow.

KEY TAKEAWAYS

This book streamlines tricky concepts of Human Life Value and life-time cash flow management so you can take action on your finances. I wrote this book to simplify big concepts so families can reset the way they think about their money and feel empowered to build their wealth. Here's what I want you to remember:

» It's very easy to steal from your future self if you're not careful, so you want to give your future self a seat at the table when making decisions.

» Traditional budgets fail because they are a snapshot of the present month rather than a tool to manage cash flow across decades.

» Your Human Life Value is finite: one day, your access to income will end and you will permanently transition into living on your savings.

» Income from your middle earning years must also pay for the final decades of your life; your current income needs to do double-duty.

» A consistent 20 percent savings rate *year over year* makes a comfortable life possible for your future self.

» The One-Number Budget prioritizes wealth building and simplifies your financial decision-making: you just need to live within your One Number.

» Beware of advertisers and retailers who want you to ignore the long-term impacts of increased monthly spending.

» Our loved ones' wants and needs are hard to say no to, but you need to be the adult in the room who stays financially strong. Your decisions today will help keep your whole family secure in the future.

» Building self-awareness about your own spending psychology will help you make more logical, future-oriented decisions about your money to live within your One Number.

» Developing a clear vision of the future and aligning your financial plan to achieve it is the best way to create the life you want, both right now and for your future self.

DECISION TIME

In this book, I've outlined the problems that most people have with traditional budgets and the financial advice that is built around them. I've also provided you with the best tool I know to help you solve those problems: the One-Number Budget. This solution is designed to help you include your future self in all your decision-making and allow you to live a life of independence, dignity, and enjoyment.

All that's left for you to do is also the most important thing: you need to commit.

Are you going to commit to the cash flow practices that will lead to growing the money mountain that will provide for you during your Final 30 years?

Your future self is out there, counting on you to come through for them. It's up to you to get it done.

Once you make your commitment, it's time to take action. In the following section, I've laid out a 120-Day Challenge to help launch you into positive money habits using the One-Number Budget.

You can do it.

And I'll be cheering for you and your family every step of the way!

THE 120-DAY CHALLENGE

The One-Number Budget is an incredible tool, but only if you use it. Now it's time to put it to the test with the 120-Day Challenge. Here's your mission:

1. **Calculate your one number:** Download the One-Number Budget Worksheet at onenumberbudget.com/worksheet and fill it in with your numbers. Take the time to check those pay stubs and mortgage statements to make sure your One Number is accurate.

2. **Assess your savings rate:** If your current savings rate is less than 20 percent, it's time to make some choices. What can you do right now to increase it? Remember, we're looking for steady progress, not perfection. Try bumping it up by a percentage point or two to see if you can live within a slightly smaller One Number as you work your way to your savings goal.

3. **Capture your 20 percent savings:** If your savings rate is already at 20 percent—or if you can get there without any trouble—great! Make sure that your 20 percent savings is automatically directed into your retirement fund and invested. If you're not sure how to automate this, talk to your HR rep or investment advisor to get the job done.

4. **Live within your one number:** For the next four months, give the One-Number Budget a whirl. Practice managing to your One Number and see how it feels. You can do anything for a few months!

5. **Invite friends to join the challenge:** Building a community to support you and keep you accountable will help you stay on track. Share this book and start a group where you can compare notes about your progress and talk through your feelings and any challenges that come up.

6. **Work with a financial coach:** If you already work with a financial advisor, show them your One-Number Budget worksheet and ask for help increasing your savings rate and/or investing your savings in a way that will best help you reach your vision of the future. If you don't already work with someone, please reach out to me at https://www.cranefinancial.com/. If I can't work with you myself, I'll direct you to someone who can.

At the end of your 120-Day Challenge, it's time to take stock. Were you able to live within your One Number? How did it feel? What can you do to dial up your savings rate a bit more for the next four months? How does it feel to have boosted your savings rate and have more wealth for your future self?

If you've never approached your finances as a cash flow manager before, the One-Number Budget has the potential to change your life. It puts your future first in a way that no traditional budget can. So give it a try. One day, your future self will thank you for it.

APPENDIX

Full Cost Comparison of Buying a New Car Every 5 Years vs. Every 7 Years

Amount Financed: **$30,000**
Finance Rate: **2.99%**
LOC Rate: **6.50%**

Months of Loan: **60**
Monthly Payment: **($537.59)**
Annual (Monthly x 12): **$6,451**

Difference at Age 64: **$180,547**

Buy a new car every 5 years and finance for 5 years				Buy a new car every 7 years and finance for 5 years (2 years no payment)			
AGE	CAR #	YEARS	COST	AGE	CAR #	YEARS	COST
30		1	$6,451	30		1	$6,451
31		2	$13,321	31		2	$13,321
32		3	$20,638	32		3	$20,638
33		4	$28,431	33		4	$28,431
34	1	5	$36,730	34		5	$36,730
35		1	$45,568	35		6	$39,117
36		2	$54,982	36	1	7	$41,660
37		3	$65,006	37		1	$50,819
38		4	$75,683	38		2	$60,573
39	2	5	$87,053	39		3	$70,962
40		1	$99,163	40		4	$82,025
41		2	$112,059	41		5	$93,808
42		3	$125,794	42		6	$99,905
43		4	$140,422	43	2	7	$106,399
44	3	5	$156,001	44		1	$119,766
45		1	$172,592	45		2	$134,002
46		2	$190,261	46		3	$149,163
47		3	$209,079	47		4	$165,310
48		4	$229,120	48		5	$182,506
49	4	5	$250,464	49		6	$194,369
50		1	$273,195	50	3	7	$207,003
51		2	$297,404	51		1	$226,909
52		3	$323,187	52		2	$248,110
53		4	$350,645	53		3	$270,688
54	5	5	$379,888	54		4	$294,733
55		1	$411,031	55		5	$320,342
56		2	$444,200	56		6	$341,164
57		3	$479,524	57	4	7	$363,340
58		4	$517,144	58		1	$393,408
59	6	5	$557,209	59		2	$425,431
60		1	$599,879	60		3	$459,535
61		2	$645,322	61		4	$495,856
62		3	$693,719	62		5	$534,537
63		4	$745,262	63		6	$575,733
64	7	5	$800,155	64	5	7	$619,607

Figure 14: Hypothetical example for illustrative purposes only.

This material has not been endorsed by Guardian, its subsidiaries, agents, or employees. No representation or warranty, either express or implied, is provided in relation to the accuracy, completeness, or reliability of the information contained herein. In addition, the content does not necessarily represent the opinions of Guardian, its subsidiaries, agents, or employees. This material is intended for general public use. By providing this content, Park Avenue Securities LLC is not undertaking to provide investment advice or a recommendation for any specific individual or situation, or to otherwise act in a fiduciary capacity. Please contact a financial representative for guidance and information that is specific to your individual situation. All scenarios and names mentioned herein are purely fictional and have been created solely for training purposes. Any resemblance to existing situations, persons, or fictional characters is coincidental. The information presented should not be used as the basis for any specific investment advice.

John Crane is a Registered Representative and Financial Advisor of Park Avenue Securities LLC (PAS). OSJ: 11350 McCormick Rd, Executive Plaza III, Suite 202, Hunt Valley, MD, 21031, 667-318-0801. Securities products and advisory services offered through PAS, member FINRA, SIPC. Financial Representative of The Guardian Life Insurance Company of America® (Guardian), New York, NY. PAS is a wholly owned subsidiary of Guardian. Crane Financial LLC is not an affiliate or subsidiary of PAS or Guardian. CA Insurance License Number - 0G79065. 2022-134740 Exp 03/24

ACKNOWLEDGMENTS

The list of people that helped me as I've moved through life is long. My editor said there wasn't enough room to list every name, so please forgive me if you feel left out.

I'd like to thank my parents Wallace and Julia Crane, who gave my sister and me the gift of a childhood where we could just be kids while they took care of all the adult stuff.

To my sister Elizabeth, who gave me another incredible gift. While I was still in high school, you gave me a copy of Robert G. Allen's *Creating Wealth* for Christmas, which planted the seeds for my future career.

To Coach Michael Gulino for his leadership as head coach of the Byram Hills High School track team. You generously gave me a formula for how to be successful, not just on the track, but also in life. I will be forever grateful that you were there during my high school years and that you continue to be there during my adult life.

To my childhood neighbor, Charles Shapiro, who hired me at the age of 15 to work in his real estate consulting business. You even took me on a sales call in lower Manhattan to meet with a senior vice president at one of the largest banks in the world. Your faith in me gave me the confidence to do things in business that I'm not sure I would have attempted if not for that first opportunity.

My first career was in the telecommunications industry, and I'm thankful for all of the managers that gave me a job: Douglas Doller, Joseph Kelly, Donald Kahn, Tammy Leppo, Larry Daldin, Tom Clarke, Gary Austin, Ron Pyles, and Mike Boyland. Each of you placed a brick that became the strong foundation for my career in the financial services industry. Thank you all for hiring me and teaching me!

To Dr. Jim Poisant, my marketing professor at George Mason University. I'm grateful to you for taking the time to meet me for breakfast at the Silver Diner in Tysons to help me figure out what I was going to do with my career. That meeting helped me find my way to a career in the financial services industry, which was better aligned with my personality, strengths, and natural curiosities.

To the leaders in the financial services industry that trained me to help people with their money decisions: Quincy Crawford, John Dixon, Joseph DeLisi, Leonard Raskin, Mike Spicer, Ben Geber, Marwan Jabbour, Marc DiFiore, Art Sanger, Bob Castiglone, Bob Ball, Steve Miller, Vincent D'Addona, and Mark Matson. Over the past 20 years, all of you generously shared your experiences and knowledge, which enabled me to then serve hundreds of nice families in a special way. Thank you for helping me build a career grounded in truth and in serving others.

To Joe DeLisi, my friend and colleague in the financial services industry. For the past 20 years we helped each other navigate all of the opportunities and challenges that come with getting started and working in the financial services industry. I don't know how anyone could make it through without a trusted colleague and friend like you.

I've been blessed with a number of close friendships over the decades: Paul and Mike Nickolas, who I spent so much time with growing up that I feel we are more brothers than friends; J. Todd Ross, who hosted one of the most eventful rounds of golf I ever played at Fort Belvoir; Pastor Dale Seley and Pastor Dan Carlton, for helping me find and follow the path of Christ Jesus; Andy Blocker, my friend and an absolute Cleaner through and through; Penn Ketchum, my Wrench Brother in endurance sports and in life; Mike Stein, who started out as a great contact for residential mortgages and quickly became a great friend; and Andrew Frutiger, with whom I spent many hours solving the world's problems in our dorm room at Susquehanna University.

To Dan Sullivan and the team at Strategic Coach®, for providing the tools and the accountability to drive me ever closer to living in my Unique Ability®. Thank you for sharing your thinking tools with the world. I believe that I progressed further and faster than I would have had it not been for your books, facilitators, and my classmates.

And most importantly:

To the nice families I'm blessed to serve as clients. Without you, I wouldn't have a career that lets me spend my days serving others. Thank you for choosing me as your advisor.

ABOUT THE AUTHOR

JOHN CRANE is a Financial Advisor providing retirement income planning to the nicest families anyone could ever hope to serve. In 2021, he was named Top of Table by MDRT, the Premier Association of Financial Professionals. John is also the author of *Healthy Money: Making a Successful Transition from Resident to Attending*, a financial guide for physicians completing their medical training.

When he's not busy helping clients understand how to build and protect their wealth, John can be found training for his next race. An avid runner, John has completed nine marathons and the inaugural MCM Urban Ultra 50K. He's also happy to slow things down and spend time with his wife and daughter in their home in Alexandria, Virginia.

Made in the USA
Las Vegas, NV
19 January 2024

84607691R00111